Dirty Deeds Done Cheap

Pete Mercer

Dirty Deeds Done Cheap

The Incredible Story of My Life from the SBS to a Hired Gun in Iraq

JOHN BLAKE

Published by John Blake Publishing Ltd,
3 Bramber Court, 2 Bramber Road,
London W14 9PB, UK

www.blake.co.uk

First published in hardback in 2008

ISBN: 978-1-84454-628-2

British Library Cataloguing-in-Publication Data:
A catalogue record for this book is available from the British Library.

Design by www.envydesign.co.uk

Printed in the UK by CPI William Clowes Beccles NR34 7TL

1 3 5 7 9 10 8 6 4 2

Text copyright © Peter Mercer, 2008

Photography © Peter Mercer

Papers used by John Blake Publishing are natural, recyclable products made from
wood grown in sustainable forests. The manufacturing processes conform to the
environmental regulations of the country of origin.

To my wonderful wife and co-writer Kim, without whose help and support this book would not have been possible.

To Morgan and Beth for tolerating me.

To my parents, Dave & Eddy and my sister Sarah with thanks for your support.

I love you all.

Last but not least to all my old team – Be Safe!

Contents

Chapter 1

Something to Do

After serving eight years in the Royal Marine Commandos, for three of which I was attached to the Special Forces Support Group, Special Boat Service, I was an ideal candidate for work as a private military contractor. After the Marines, I'd been mainly working in the oil industry in Nigeria and Trinidad doing weld inspection jobs, and, to tell you the truth, my life was getting a little dull. The money was great but the job could be mundane at the best of times and utterly miserable at others.

I still undertook the occasional security job and one of those jobs combined both the oil industry and security work. This was out in Nigeria, and I was working on one of their oil rigs. It was a bit of an eye opener.

Nigeria has only recently discovered oil in its coastal waters and has started drilling for it. However, the ordinary Nigerians are extremely poor. Because these people are so poor, they sometimes try to tap into the oil pipelines to get fuel, often with disastrous consequences. They have even used blowtorches to cut open these pipelines and the resulting explosions take out scores of people every time. It seems, however, that these poor souls never learn from their mistakes, since it happens with appalling regularity.

The other main way to make money for the ordinary Nigerian is kidnap for ransom and piracy. When I was working in Nigeria we had an armed escort to take us from the airport to our hotels and from the hotels to the heliport for onward transportation to the rigs. White people are always a target out there and armed gangs have been known to kidnap people travelling around the country. There really is no exploring this country: it just wouldn't be safe.

In my job in Nigeria I had two main roles. One was to search the arrivers and leavers – the leavers especially because they were a light-fingered bunch who would steal anything they could lay their hands on and then try to smuggle it off the rig. I even caught people trying to nick computers – which aren't exactly small. Unfortunately, they weren't blessed with much in the way of brains and getting caught would result in their losing a well-paid job for trying to do something that they didn't really have a hope in hell of getting away with.

My other role was to repel pirates and kidnappers if they should attempt to board the rigs. To this end I carried a shotgun. The pirates, if they managed to get on board, would not only steal whatever they could but would also kidnap any European workers on the rig – of whom there weren't that many – and hold them for ransom. They never asked for much in the way of ransom particularly, and the oil companies generally paid up – so it could work out quite profitable for these pirates. It was a very boring job but it paid well and the climate was nice and hot – I love hot places!

Anyway, back to my story. I'd just arrived back from Nigeria in January 2004. My normal routine was to land at the airport, get home, shag the missus and go out and get pissed – though not necessarily in that order.

This particular weekend I'd got home, and, as soon as I entered the room, the missus and I had a massive fight, so I thought, Fuck it – I don't need this shit! I packed a bag, jumped in the car and drove up to London to see some old squaddie mates, hopefully for a great piss-up. My missus threw a massive wobbler and I knew then it was over, since we were arguing all the time. When you're working away so much, often all you want to do is get out and have a drink and chill before you get home, but this can certainly cause rifts at home. It certainly did this time, but I was up for ending it anyway. The relationship was going sour and I'd fallen out of love. It had run its course, that was for sure.

I got to London early that Friday night and rang around all the lads. Stevie was the only one out and about, which I was a bit pissed off about, but Stevie was a great laugh and up for anything – a nice nutter if you like. I'd met up once with Stevie in a dwarf whorehouse in Malaysia where you could do dwarf throwing. Basically, in this place a dwarf in a Velcro suit ran up to you and you picked them up and chucked them against a prickly wall. I'd only just walked into the place and bumped into Stevie and, while Stevie was trying to talk to me over a pint, this dwarf kept hounding him, so Stevie turned round and picked him up and lobbed him against the wall. But it was the wrong fucking wall. No Velcro! The dwarf smashed against a painting and then hit the deck with a thud. We had to leave pretty sharpish. It was a pure accident but the proprietor didn't see it that way. In this place you could even get a dwarf shag if you were that way inclined (and Stevie was!).

Stevie was an ex-SAS guy that I'd met while doing a survival course with the SAS back in 1993. He was a Scot, slight of build but a tough little cookie, who reminded me of a terrier. He was a good friend of mine and a great guy. Anyway, I got to his house and we reminisced about work over a beer or two for a while, and then decided to hit the town. This was always going to be eventful, my main mission for the evening being to keep Stevie fully clothed. He had an embarrassing habit of getting naked at every opportunity when drunk – a typical ex-bootneck (or Royal Marine Commando – see Glossary for this and other terminology).

We hit all the pubs and clubs we were allowed into and this is pretty much the last thing I remember. It was a hectic boozy night and Stevie nearly got us nicked when he decided to piss behind a lamppost on the way home, but the coppers who turned up were surprisingly OK. He got a bollocking and was let off. We staggered off back to Stevie's place, stopping by a kebab house on the way home. Why is it that when you get drunk kebabs taste like heaven?

We woke up at Stevie's the next morning with stinking hangovers and had a beer and a bacon butty for breakfast, after I'd had a shower and wiped all the previous night's kebab off my face. The postman called and Stevie opened his mail. I was intrigued when he jumped into the air and gave it a '*Yes!*' He explained that he'd applied for a job working as a bodyguard in Baghdad for £750 per day and he'd got the job. He was off in one week. This totally got my brain ticking over and I thought, What the hell! I wouldn't mind a bit of that myself. So I got details of all the companies that Stevie had applied to (mainly based in London, the USA and South Africa) and secured some interviews.

The next Wednesday I turned up at one of the offices of a major security company in London. I was interviewed by a former high-ranking soldier who was working as the recruitment and selection guy for this particular company. His job was to vet the potential private soldiers to assess our suitability for whatever jobs the company had. He told me that they employed around three thousand guys working all over the world, but that work in Iraq was paying the best rates at this time, so that's what I went for.

After some pretty serious questioning and a series of security checks and references, I was told I could be off to Baghdad on that Friday! I was slightly in shock, to say the least, but I was certainly up for it. I'd never earned this sort of money (£500 a day) in my life and probably was unlikely ever to again – if I lived to spend it!

I jumped in the motor and hammered it home to the West Country to give the good news to my now becalmed girlfriend, Victoria. She wasn't calm for long when I told her my news. She went fucking mental and called me all the names she could think of and some I'd never heard of before (though I think she probably made them up). This took quite a long time and I interrupted her only when she started to repeat herself.

She was in shock and asked me how long I'd be away for and if I really thought I'd get back in one piece. Typically, being a bloke, I just grumbled 'Don't know' to pretty much every question she asked. In fact she must have asked about a hundred questions but I hadn't been told much myself and just gave the same two-word answer over and over again, which really pissed her off.

All I knew was that I would be based at Baghdad Airport and I would be responsible for escorting clients from the airport to the Green Zone (the supposedly secure area) in Baghdad. Also, there was going to be the job of securing the perimeter. This was going to be done by working alongside three hundred ex-Gurkha soldiers who would be mounted in machine-gun posts every few hundred metres. That was all I knew at this particular moment. But what the hell! I had to look on the bright side: at least it was going to be nice and warm – and I might even get a suntan!

Back home, I did the usual on the Thursday evening and went out for a few pints with some mates and got a bit wasted – but not *too* wasted.

Friday morning I woke up with a banging hangover and could barely lift my head off the pillow, but reality gave me a rude awakening. I was off to Iraq very shortly.

There were plenty of tears from Victoria as I packed my stuff, but I still managed to sweet-talk her into driving me to London – I think she secretly wanted to take me, anyway. After sitting in the car with her for over two hours packed with horrible silences broken only by bitchy comments from her and pronouncements of impending doom and disaster that she said I'd definitely encounter, I finally wished I'd caught the train.

We arrived at the head office in London and there were more tears from Victoria. I gave her a hug and a small peck on the cheek then waved goodbye. I watched her drive away and wondered if I'd done the right thing, taking on this mental job. Oh well, I was here now so I'd best get on with it.

As I approached the impressively huge building that was their headquarters, I was reminded of one of the opening scenes from the film *The Wild Geese*. I pressed the buzzer to gain entrance. It was 10 a.m. and I was soon in the office signing my life away: contracts, life insurance, next of kin and a will (I left everything to my dad).

By twelve o'clock I was off to London Heathrow to catch my flight out. It was only when I was on the train that my mind started turning over. I'd never been to Baghdad before. I'd been serving with the Royal Marine Commandos during the First Gulf War but we were based in northern Iraq, clearing positions of the Republican Guard, and we hadn't come anywhere near the capital. I wouldn't say I was nervous, just intrigued.

I hadn't had time to do my homework on Baghdad much, but I'd called some mates who had worked out there and a couple who actually were working out there and encountered mixed feelings from those I managed to speak to. Apparently, some of the companies that guys I knew worked for really looked after you, supplying you with good weapons, good healthcare, good insurance and so forth. However, some of the companies gave little backup and, if you got in the shit, you were *really* in the shit!

After all the paperwork was taken care of I had a coffee and just sat around and talked to one of the girls in the office. This company must have had a policy of just hiring lovely women because the office was full of them. A short while later I was out of the building and on my way.

Once at the terminal at Heathrow I looked on the display screen for my flight to Schiphol Airport, Amsterdam, as this was to be my first stop. I then grabbed a newspaper and went to the bar and ordered myself a cup of coffee.

Around that time (January 2004) there was still a hell of a lot of stuff in the papers about Iraq and especially Baghdad. I read it all with immense interest.

The time in the airport flew by and I was soon on the first

leg of what would be a trip that would change my life in so many ways.

After arriving in Schiphol I quickly located the flight display screen and looked for the next leg of my journey; I discovered I had four hours to wait. This was going to be no problem, as I find Schiphol fascinating. It's huge and very cosmopolitan and you can buy anything there. The shopping is great and, of course, it's tax-free.

Before long my flight to Kuwait was announced and I proceeded to Departures. I got on the flight and by now I was feeling some trepidation. However, old habits die hard and I had been a Royal Marine Commando for nearly nine years and had learned to grab some sleep whenever I could – before long I was in the land of Nod.

I was awoken by the stewardess asking me to fasten my seatbelt as we were coming in to land. I'd slept for hours and was a little bit disoriented at first, but I soon came round. As we flew over Kuwait I could see the lights of all the high-rise buildings that towered above the rest of the city. As I left the aircraft I had to take off my jacket because of the stifling heat, which hit you like a brick wall as soon as you left the comfort of the air conditioning. This place was hot!

After clearing customs I casually looked around for my contact, who was to meet me and take me to the company's headquarters in Kuwait City. I had no idea what he looked like, so this was a bit futile. I was standing around like a lemon outside the terminal and feeling a bit edgy when this big six-foot guy with a moustache and definite military bearing approached me. I knew straightaway that this must be my contact.

'Hi, Pete,' he said. He had a picture of me from a scan of my passport sent ahead from London, so he knew what I looked like. He guided me out of the airport to a waiting car. It was nice to get into the air-con. We drove to the hotel where the company had an office and we talked all the way. His name was Tom, but he couldn't enlighten me as to exactly what I would be doing because he wasn't privy to that sort of information. He explained that his only job was to take care of the admin, get us in and out of Iraq and to repatriate the bodies of the guys who were killed, which was, worryingly, quite a few.

The office was a large, converted, five-star hotel apartment on the coast of Kuwait. It was full of computers, printers and fax machines. I could see only two young females of European origin, who seemed to be the only members of staff present. There were piles of body armour and helmets in the corner of the office. I assumed this was to be used for getting in and out of Iraq.

Although by this time it was quite late, the place was still buzzing. I could see they had a great view from the patio doors, which looked out over a beautiful man-made bay. It was floodlit outside and I could see that it was still really busy, with lots of people out for an evening stroll. The beach looked fantastic and I wondered if I'd get a chance to have a closer look.

I was standing gazing out of the window when one of the girls at the office came over and issued me with a meal ticket. I went down the stairs and across the beach to the restaurant. The restaurant was charming and the waitresses were all very beautiful Asian women. I had the most fantastic fillet steak I've ever eaten in my life. I lingered there for a while, digesting my meal and drinking coffee and just soaking up the atmosphere – but hanging around in a restaurant by yourself gets boring, so I returned to the office. I was given a small brief and some travelling instructions. We were to leave at 06.00 to travel to an American airbase on the border of Iraq and Kuwait. I was now well and truly on my way.

After a restless evening with not much sleep I was up at 05.00 and grabbed some breakfast. I met up with Tom, who asked if I'd got everything I needed – passport and travel documents, etc. It was then that I noticed two other guys sitting in the corner of the office. One was a short stocky American with muscles on his muscles – he obviously spent a lot of time in the gym pushing weights. He was introduced to me as Dwight (his nickname was Hollywood – fuck knows why). The other man was a tall muscular French guy who was introduced to me as Phillipe. Dwight was an ex-US Marine, Phillipe was ex-French Foreign Legion.

We had a brief chat and it turned out that Dwight was travelling to Baghdad with me, while Phillipe was heading up to the north of Iraq on what seemed to me and everyone else to be a suicide mission from what I could gather from the briefing, but it was one I would soon find very familiar.

After a morning brief, we all loaded our kitbags, body armour and helmets into the back of a station wagon and set off for the Kuwait–Iraq border. Tom drove. As we travelled along we passed many damaged buildings, some of which been partly destroyed. It turned out that the damage had been done during the First Gulf War and had yet to be fully repaired. For an oil-rich country earning billions, you would have thought that thirteen years on they would have got around to fixing the place up; this, obviously, wasn't the case. There seemed to be a lot of poverty, which I found to be quite shocking.

After about two hours of driving we arrived at a crossroads. We then turned right down a dusty track and drove for another two kilometres until we came to a US military checkpoint. Tom produced his ID card and then we all had to get out of the vehicle for a security search. We then all had to produce our travel documents and passports.

The US Army Military Police searched the vehicle for weapons and hidden explosives and held us while they confirmed our identities. Obviously, we did not fit the profile of a terrorist or insurgent. However, it had been known for journalists and black-marketeers to try to gain access to American bases using the excuse of being private military contractors.

We passed all the security checks then we got back into our vehicle and continued on to the airbase. Eventually, we saw what can only be described as a huge airport in the middle of the desert. There were military hangars everywhere and all types of aircraft – military, civilian and obviously CIA (they had the shiny civilian choppers).

On arriving at the terminal car park, I saw that there were all kinds of vehicles, from military tanks and armoured vehicles down to normal Ford cars. There were US troops everywhere getting ready to deploy into Iraq and in among these troops were quite a few private military contractors – or PMCs. I looked around hoping to spot some familiar faces but I couldn't see any.

Inside the terminal was a young US army sergeant who was acting as some sort of customs officer. He checked our bags and then our paperwork again. Everything was in order and we were cleared for transport to Baghdad. The terminal was a massive hustle and bustle of activity, which could be best described as organised chaos.

Tom wished us good luck and said his goodbyes and wandered off leaving us to stew in the sweltering heat, which was now up to near 40 degrees Celsius. We all fell silent, as I guess most of us were feeling a bit tense and apprehensive. Even the young soldiers we saw were strangely quiet. I guessed that some of them were getting ready for their first tour of duty in Iraq. I felt for them – they looked so young. It reminded me of the time when I had shipped out for the First Gulf War when I was twenty years old, excited but nervous at the same time.

We waited, sweating our tits off, in the terminal for four

hours, downing water like something that was going out of fashion. We'd still not acclimatised properly, as we'd been in the country for less than two days and had left England in freezing, rainy weather to come here, where it was 35–40 degrees Celsius. Eventually, at 12.30 that afternoon, we were summoned for our flight into Baghdad. We fell into line with what must have been about fifty American Marines, all armed to the teeth. Phillipe, Dwight and I donned our body armour and helmets and climbed aboard the back of a waiting truck. Some of the obviously new Marines looked as us with astonishment, not knowing who we were, but nobody asked us any questions. Various agencies working for different governments travel in and out of Iraq every day – but this was apparently new to a lot of them.

We drove across the runway to a waiting C-130 Hercules transport aircraft. It was the first time in a while that I'd been in a Herc and it was quite nostalgic. Phillipe, Dwight and I boarded last, so we were right next to the tailgate. All the US Marines had their packs between their legs, some looking more than a little nervous. I hoped that I didn't look as apprehensive, because some of these guys really looked as if they were shitting it. I told myself that, since I had travelled in and out of quite a few war zones in my time, I knew pretty much what to expect, so I hoped that I looked a bit more confident.

The heat inside the aircraft was stifling and I couldn't wait to get going and get airborne so we could get a bit of a through draught. I could feel the sweat running down my shirt as my body armour acted like a body *warmer*. We started to taxi for what seemed like an eternity, then the pilot gunned the throttles and we started to accelerate very rapidly. Because everyone who is a passenger in a Herc has to sit sideways we were all fighting to stay upright, against the g-force. They really pack those Hercs – I figured I knew how a sardine felt.

The plane climbed steeply and, even with my ear defenders on, the noise was still pretty deafening until the plane eventually flattened out at terminal altitude and the pilot throttled off and the noise decreased to a drone. Within a matter of minutes almost everyone was asleep.

As a young Royal Marine Commando I'll never forget the feeling I had when I was on my first basic parachute course. You're absolutely shitting yourself but for some strange reason the resonance, hum and vibration of the aircraft sends you to sleep. It's almost hypnotic.

We were awoken by one of our neighbouring Marines nudging us as the loadmaster signalled that we were approaching Baghdad. Since there only a few windows in a C-130 – and we weren't sitting anywhere near those because they are at the front – no one could see anything. All we had was the smell of aviation fuel and the hypnotic hum.

We had learned, through the grapevine, that two weeks previously during an identical landing two guys were shot and killed in the back of one of these Hercs by insurgent snipers, so I was just praying that I wouldn't get shot in the arse. What a way to go: done through the arse!

Just then the pilot banked hard to port and we all hung on for dear life. He then banked hard to starboard. All the time the aircraft was losing altitude at an alarming rate. We were almost weightless in the back. Everyone had now passed looking apprehensive and was bordering on shitting himself. The landing gear was soon down and within minutes we had made a perfect landing; we then all relaxed a little.

It turns out that the insurgents had been studying certain landmarks on the flight path into Baghdad International Airport and used them to work out when to fire at incoming Coalition aircraft. Sneaky bastards! All the pilot had been doing was trying to mess this up for them. I wished he had shared this information with us before take-off. It would have saved a few pairs of soiled underpants I'm sure.

Under hard braking and the roar of the engines' reverse-thrusting we came to a halt. There was a whine of the turbines as the pilot shut down the engines and the tailgate came down. As it did so a glorious smell of aviation fuel filled the plane; I fucking love that smell.

We were now in Baghdad. I got off the plane and it was now that I was wondering whether I'd done the right thing, taking on this crazy job. We picked up our kit and walked down the ramp. I could see a white Toyota Hilux coming across the runway towards us. Behind me I could hear a US Marine drill sergeant bellowing at his men to fall in. It reminded me of being back in the mob. Discipline is so very necessary in the military because, when you have to move and take these young men into battle, there can be no room for error. When you say jump all they must do is ask, 'How high?' This isn't always nice, but it is a necessity. The chain of command is essential. As PMCs, we didn't always have or need this, as we knew we were mostly on our own, but for the regular armed forces it is vital.

The Hilux pulled up next to us and a small blond-haired guy jumped out. All he was dressed in were shorts and a T-shirt with a pistol on his waist. I couldn't believe that he wore no body armour. We all thought that this was odd, being in the middle of Iraq and all. He introduced himself as Bruce and we all piled into the Hilux and off we went.

We drove for what seemed like quite a few miles before going through a few checkpoints. He explained to us that Baghdad airport was 45 square miles and was protected by fifty-thousand American troops and three-thousand PMCs. We all felt a bit more secure and could see why he carried only a pistol. He explained to us that apparently it wasn't policy to wear body armour unless you were near the perimeter of the airport. We sped back across the runway and into a car park. The car park was packed with PMCs all waiting to pick up their new guys, clients or men coming back off leave. Meanwhile, we could see that there were Hercs landing all of the time. This place was very busy.

We then drove past one of Saddam Hussein's impressive summer palaces, which it turns out I would later be living in, and all kinds of fantastic palatial buildings that Saddam had had built for his military hierarchy. They at least had been well treated, for there were swimming pools and quite a few Jacuzzis for their use. While the tyrant had been in power, he had taken all the farmers' land and water supplies to use for his own private boating lakes and so, after the Second Gulf War, once Saddam had been overthrown, the farmers had taken all of this back and all of his lakes and pools were now dried up as the farmers had diverted the water and used it for their irrigation systems. Good on them, I say!

As we drove along Bruce was giving us a running commentary about what Dwight and I would be doing. It turned out that Bruce was the company doctor. He said he didn't know what Phillipe would be doing but could only say he would be going up north and he thought that it was dodgy. In fact it was going to be very dangerous indeed. The north of Iraq was, and still is, a no-go area for most PMCs. The north is well known as an insurgent stronghold and to work up there you learned to expect the worse.

After a twenty-minute drive, past quite a few runways and impressive buildings, we pulled up outside a large tent. Bruce informed us that this was one of the many American chow tents (as they were known) and we could get something to eat here. Bruce cleared his pistol as we entered the compound (basically, he took the magazine off, cocked it and made sure that there was no round in the chamber) and then we went in. It was a big no-no to take a loaded weapon into the chow tent. Inside it was organised chaos with hungry soldiers and PMCs all getting their meals and talking all at the same time. We were all starving, though, and the scran – the food – smelled great.

We helped ourselves, and it was surprisingly good – a lot better than I remembered from my time when I was in the mob. I was looking around the tent – just being nosy, really – when I spotted a familiar face. I immediately got up and walked over to him. He was a guy called Lee I used to be in the Royal Marine Commandos with. Lee was working for a different company from mine, and told me that, apart from doing bodyguard work in Baghdad, he was also training the Iraqi police, which I thought sounded quite interesting.

Lee and I chewed the fat for a while and he gave me a number to get hold of him on. Lee was a really nice quiet guy and you would never believe that he was a bodyguard or ex-Marine, since he was a very passive and easy-going sort.

After quite a pleasant lunch, Bruce came over and told me that it was time to go. We left the chow tent and after a short drive we arrived at a compound surrounded by a tall fence with razor wire along the top and machine-gun posts every 50 metres or so.

On the gate were two guards carrying M16 assault rifles and a mounted M240 GPMG (general-purpose machine gun). They looked Nepalese and were obviously ex-Gurkhas. About 90 per cent of security companies in Iraq employed ex-Gurkhas or ex-Fijian army, and there were also quite a few Peruvians working out there. These guys are a lot cheaper to employ than Western expats and are very reliable, which helped the companies to keep their costs down (and almost certainly profits up).

We drove into the compound, which contained around fifty temporary huts, some accommodation, some stores and some offices. We pulled up and I looked around with interest, for this was going to be my base, my home, for how long I didn't know.

We went to see the camp boss, who was an ex-colonel in the British Army, and introduced ourselves. He made us feel welcome and, after a quick chat and a cup of tea, we were assigned our billets and packed our stuff away. I had a quick look around the camp. The accommodation was sparse: just a bunk bed and a couple of steel lockers. There was also an air-conditioning unit, which was working but was noisy as hell – this wasn't going to make for a pleasant stay, I thought – but I decided that for fourteen grand a month I could live with it. This was going to be home for the foreseeable future. I sat down on one of the bunks and contemplated what I'd got myself into.

We were told that there was no rank structure on camp but we did have a project manager who had overall command. He was South African and I would meet him in the morning; but for now I was advised to get my head down. I turned the air conditioning up and quickly fell asleep.

I woke up at 06.00, had a shower, grabbed my joining paperwork and went for a walk round. There was no one about! I wandered about in a bit of a daze, as I'd not got my bearings yet. I eventually found the project manager, who seemed to be nursing a stinking hangover. He asked me who I was and I told him I was one of the new guys; he told me, after a brief chat, I was to go and see the store man who would issue me with some kit.

I went off and eventually found the stores. The store man looked as rough as fuck. He'd apparently been on the piss with the project manager the previous night. He asked me what weapons I wanted. I chose a Glock 19 pistol and M16 M4 assault rifle. The Glock 19 is a great pistol, if a little too small for my big hands, but it was either that or a Browning high-power, and in the past I've had stoppages with the Browning. Besides, the Glocks were brand-new, and everyone likes shiny new kit!

Later that day I went to meet the rest of my team and check out the vehicles we would be using. I was introduced to another expat, named Mike. Mike was team leader and in overall command. The rest of the team were to be ex-Fijian army guys. The vehicles we were using were two armoured Toyota Shoguns and one armoured American SUV (sport utility vehicle). These vehicles could withstand some minor roadside bombs and most types of gunfire. The two Toyotas would travel front and rear with the SUV in the middle. The SUV would have the client (or clients) inside; the Toyotas were for protection – gun buses, basically.

Our main task would be to take the clients off the planes that landed in Baghdad International and then escort them and pass them over to their own bodyguard teams. We would then ride alongside them in the Shoguns to provide a bit of added protection. The reason our team wasn't part of the actual bodyguard team was that Mike and I were the only PSD (personal security detachment)-trained guys; most of the Fijians were not. The PSD teams were normally ex-British Army or ex-Royal Marines Commandos.

Before I could start work in Iraq I had to get my American ID card. This could be a right pain in the arse to get sometimes. This had to be carried with you at all times to enable you to get in and around US bases. It was going to take a week to get my ID, so I spent my spare time doing dry drills with the team (practising convoy protection) around the airport, going on the range and generally getting up to speed with procedures and getting as prepared as possible. Knowing your team and practising together is very important: the better you know how each other works, the more effective you'll be when the shit hits the fan. And in Iraq the shit would, at one stage or another, hit the fan.

The following week, my American ID arrived and the first mission I was to take part in came through. Mike called us into the office and gave us our brief. We were to pick up the client from the plane and then take him to the outskirts of the airport. At the checkpoint, Checkpoint 1, he would then be handed over to his new PSD team; our SUV would then be dropped off. He would have to get out then. This could potentially be the most dodgy part of the operation, but we had concrete hangars where this could be done in relative safety, as it would be almost impossible for an insurgent sniper to pick him off. Their two-vehicle convoy would then join with our two vehicles, we'd do a comms check and go over the routes, so that everyone was crystal clear about what was going to happen, then proceed along Route Irish (the popular name for the Baghdad Airport road).

Route Irish is probably, or at least was, the most dangerous road in the world. There were daily bombings and shootings. Numerous American soldiers have been killed, along with more than a few PMCs, along this road, but, unfortunately, it's the only route from the Baghdad Green Zone to the airport, so you've got no choice. Like it or lump it, it's part of the job.

So here we were. We'd practised our drills and honed them the best we could, but that morning I must admit I was nervous. I'd heard horror stories about the road we were about to travel along. We set off from the checkpoint with trepidation. My adrenalin was flowing and everyone was buzzing; we were all ready. I asked Mike how many contacts they'd had. He reckoned about one in every tree trips. This ratio was high. I kind of hoped that, since this was my first run out, it wouldn't be that one out of three; but I wasn't really bothered because if the shit hit the fan I was ready. We were all ready.

I cocked my M16 and put on the safety, then we took off at a pretty rapid rate out of the checkpoint, but, because of the heavy armour we carried, the Land Cruisers were slightly slower (the armoured SUV was quicker because it had an uprated engine). As we travelled along Route Irish we started approaching some American convoys. You had to be extremely careful approaching the American military because they have a reputation for sometimes lighting non-military vehicles up (basically, shooting the crap out of them). Approaching fast towards them was a very bad idea, and so we slowed right down. You can't really blame them for shooting up non-military vehicles because this is what a suicide bomber would do: drive slowly up to the convoy and then, at the last minute, speed up and detonate their device and take out most of the convoy. As soon as we were given the signal to pass, we overtook the Hummers (Humvees) and gave them a cursory wave as we went past. So far, so good.

Coming into the Green Zone there was an increased military presence: lots of barriers, machine-gun nests, armoured vehicles and lookout posts. We then split off from the main convoy so that we could turn around. There was another team waiting to take over from us – their PSD guys. It was all in their hands now. We now just had to try to make it back to the airport in one piece.

As we turned around in this dangerous place we could hear some small-arms fire. I didn't think it was directed as us at first, but then the first round struck our vehicle, then another. The American gunner, on the checkpoint's machine-gun nest, then opened up and all hell broke loose. No disrespect intended, but there is nothing worse than some nineteen-year-old Marine from Alabama with a .50-calibre heavy machine gun (or .50-cal, as we tend to call them) – they can be a bit trigger-happy at the best of times, though I guess that, since they were just young frightened guys, you couldn't really blame them. We just nailed it out of there as fast as possible and tried to get out of the line of fire, and especially get out of the kill zone that we were obviously in or, more importantly, were going into.

The comms were going mad and I was told by one of the Fijians that this was apparently pretty close to where an American officer was killed (his head blown apart by a sniper) the week before. It was a known sniper hotspot. We were in a tricky situation. Our vehicle behind was then hit. As long as it was small-arms fire we would pretty much be OK because of our armour, but if they got a rocket-propelled grenade (RPG) off we'd really be in the shit. An RPG would take you out. We were now nearly in the clear but, as we were all trying to get out of the kill zone, there was a commotion on the comms again. Unbelievably, a round that had been fired by an insurgent sniper had gone between the door frame and glass, the most vulnerable point in the vehicle, and had hit the Fijian bodyguard sitting in the passenger seat of the rear vehicle. We didn't know the extent of his injuries but we couldn't stop to check or assess them because to stop would be suicide. We just knew we had to get out of there – and quick!

The rounds had stopped striking now, but we were far from out of danger, because the whole of Route Irish could be a shooting gallery. We drove as fast as possible, each of us aware of our bleeding but conscious comrade and the need to get him medical attention as soon as we could. The Fijian in the back seat was in the meantime applying pressure to his wound. As soon as we'd got past the road blocks, which were manned by American troops at Baghdad Airport (and some of our company's guys), they had a medic team waiting for us. They went straight to work on the Fijian and the paramedics got him straight into an ambulance. He had, miraculously, been hit in the shoulder, the 7.62mm round ripping out a large chunk of flesh. Those Fijians are hard bastards, mind, and he was out of hospital the next day with a shoulder full of stitches. Once we were back on camp and with our Fijian comrade being looked after, we took the Land Cruisers down to the garage to give them a good once-over. Apart from the bullet strikes, there was no real damage. Some of these vehicles cost over £100,000 each and are designed to take quite a large bomb hit.

Over the next week we did three more runs without incident.

The airport in Baghdad was a fascinating place. There were quite a few companies based there. There is a company called Triple Canopy (TC), who employ only ex-US Special Forces, and there is Blackwater, who do pretty much the same. After the war ended in 2003, Blackwater were probably one of the first PMC companies out in Iraq and, going along Route Irish, they lost an alarming number of personnel. It was their men who hit the headlines in the papers when they were dragged out of their vehicles, executed and then dragged through the streets and hung up and burned in Fallujah. This had been broadcast on TV channels across the world and was a truly shocking sight, showing what can go wrong if you get complacent or unlucky.

Baghdad – and Iraq in general – is such a volatile place. With danger lurking around every corner you must always have your wits about you. Every precaution must be taken to avoid getting ambushed or, even worse, getting trapped and boxed in down some side street. This is why route selection is so very important on jobs. To be captured would be just unimaginable.

We were based at Baghdad Airport near to Triple Canopy, and we often used to go over and visit, just for a coffee or a tea, or in the evening something stronger maybe. Early one morning Mike and I were on our way over to meet up with some of the guys from TC to go for a run. Being ex-US Special Forces, most of them are pretty fit. We set off for our run, carrying just our pistols. We were just building up a sweat and getting a pace going when we heard the familiar whine of incoming mortars. We had no cover to get behind! We were in the shit – big time. All we could do was hit the deck and hope for the best.

The first round struck some buildings nearby, shattering some of the glass and doors. When a mortar lands it is designed to explode as effectively as possible – it sends small shards of razor-sharp shrapnel in every direction and they can be lethal up to 100 metres. These things were doing just that, so we had to lie low and hope for the best.

Two more rounds dropped, roughly on the same location. We looked at each other nervously at first, then everyone got the giggles! Why is it that in situations like these you tend to laugh? When we thought that it was all clear and relatively safe, we made our move. We needed to get back to our compounds, and fast, since we weren't sure whether any more of these things were going to come down on us. I don't think any one of us had ever run so fast in his life. When we got back to the safety of our compounds, we were all knackered! I had a shower. That had been one close escape and it was certain that we'd have quite a few more to come in the future, but hopefully not when we were out for a run.

Life travelling along Route Irish and bumming around camp soon began to wear thin. I started to look around different companies for different jobs, but I soon decided it was time to go home on some leave. I was due some, so I put in a leave request and was soon off. Leave was nice and chilled, but for some weird reason it was good to come back.

When I arrived back off leave, everything workwise was pretty uneventful. I got back into camp and fell back into the routine, the normal rigmarole. I went to have a coffee with my boss and asked him if the French guy (Phillipe) had gone up north yet. He said he had. Don't ask me why, but I immediately asked for a job change. The boss gave me a frown and a slightly shifty look. 'You don't want to go up there, not unless you're not arsed about coming back in one piece or at all.' After a week of pestering I got my job change. My boss was extremely reluctant to let me go and kept asking me why I wanted to go. I couldn't tell him why I wanted to go – I just knew that I did. He eventually relented and I got ready for the off. Good move or bad move I didn't know.

I turned up at 05.00 the next morning, handed in my M16 and Glock in the stores and proceeded to the main terminal at Baghdad International Airport. At 06.30 a civilian Russian plane landed and we all proceeded to get on board. There were around thirty of us, mainly Fijians, all travelling up to Mosul. I couldn't believe it when we boarded – the plane had two pretty Russian air stewardesses on board, and after takeoff we were served with an orange juice. Here we were, flying into the most dangerous place in Iraq in a civilian airliner.

After a great takeoff and once the seat-belt signs went off, I went into the cockpit to talk to the pilots. They were both Russian and I asked them if they knew that they were flying into the most dangerous place in the world. 'We were helicopter pilots in Afghan war, Iraq no bother us,' was their answer. So here I was flying in broad daylight into the most dangerous place in the world piloted by two psycho Russian shot-to-pieces war veterans! At this time the military wouldn't even fly into Mosul in broad daylight, fearing it was too dangerous! So I went back to my seat, feeling pretty nervous (on military aircraft you at least have quite a few countermeasures against missile attacks, but on civilian aircraft you have none). I sat down and buckled in. Two hours later we were coming in to land. I was just waiting for some sort of projectile to hit us but everything went fine. In fact we could have been landing anywhere in the world and you wouldn't have known any difference. Very smooth, these pilots weren't fazed by anything. They were proper headcases.

As soon as we landed the steps came up to the main door and we emerged into the bright sunshine. At the bottom of the steps a flatbed truck was waiting for us. Our kit was offloaded in double-quick time and we chucked all of it onto the back and then all piled on. This was Mosul Airport, one of the most dodgy airports on the planet! It was a very small airport, which had been taken over by the American military as an airstrip to fly equipment in and to supply logistics to the north of the country for their missions. It had now been turned into a huge military base.

As we travelled across the runways we came up to one of the most mental things I have ever seen: six Toyota Hiluxes with all the doors taken off (for the purpose of quick exit), all welded together with homemade armour, and in the back each vehicle had a big gun mounted – M240s, M19 grenade launchers and .50-cals! I've never seen anything like it. It looked like a scene from a *Mad Max* movie with everyone in the trucks armed to the teeth. The Hiluxes were battered and covered in bullet and shrapnel holes. I was bricking it a bit now – these guys had obviously been in a lot of action. Maybe I'd bitten off more than I could chew. Whatever, I would soon find out. I then saw Phillipe and we said our hellos.

It was now around 17.30 and I was told that we'd have to get a move on because it was even more dangerous travelling at night across Mosul than during the day for us. I was given an M16 and two thirty-round magazines, and got put in the back seat in the middle of one of the Toyotas (the safest place in one of those vehicles). Manning the machine-gun turrets in the back were Fijians and Gurkhas. Everyone was facing outwards in the trucks with their weapons at the ready. We were joined by other vehicles and formed a convoy.

The convoy drove out of camp at full throttle. I didn't know what to expect. As we went round the first bend into the town a car approached us. One of our guys put his hand up, to indicate to the driver to stop. The car still came towards us. Bang! Bang! He fired two rounds in front of the car. The car stopped. It was company policy not to actually shoot the car or its occupants unless it was absolutely necessary, but we could take no chances. We were to fire warning shots only and to kill only if it was absolutely necessary. However, there are some wankers working in Iraq who seemed just to shoot anything or anyone for fun. This is totally unprofessional and does nothing for hearts and minds. I believe it is counterproductive but, unfortunately, there are quite a few contractors in Iraq who think it's OK to open up on anything. The guys I was working with, though, were of the highest standard.

As we went through town all the guys were hard-targeting (aiming their weapons along their lines of sight), looking down side streets, looking for anywhere we could be ambushed from or shot at. It was not unknown for the insurgents to hide their bombs in absolutely anything or anywhere (even explosives concealed inside dead animals). However, the guys I was travelling with were good, very good – I could tell these were hardened veterans.

Although I was nervous and my adrenalin was sky high, everyone was so professional and focused, and I had a feeling I was going to like this job. As we travelled along, you could see holes in the road and scorch marks on walls and bridges where IEDs had gone off. There were bullet holes everywhere. This looked like a very fucking dangerous place.

I was in the rear vehicle. There was a gunner on the back with an M240 7.62mm machine gun facing backwards, ready to deal with any threat from the rear. Every now and again you could hear gunshots and the odd bang, and it was pretty unnerving for me at first, but these guys didn't even flinch. They'd obviously gone through this a thousand times before, but I hadn't.

We drove for around thirty minutes until we reached the American camp, which was going to be my new home. As we approached, I noticed that the gates had big chains and wires across, obviously to stop suicide bombers from piling on through them and accessing the camp. Big concrete bollards zigzagged up towards the entrance – this was to ensure that no suicide bombers in a car or truck had a straight run at the camp (as they did at the US Marines barracks in Beirut in 1982). Either side of the chains there were machine-gun posts, heavily armed with .50-cal weapons, which were capable of taking most things out.

The camp was totally encased by thick concrete walls with concrete shelters dotted around the place, in which you could take cover in case of mortar strikes. In Baghdad, inside the airport, it was always deadly quiet, but now, up here, it was totally different. Every now and then you could hear automatic gunfire in the distance. This was part of what was called Operation Iraqi Freedom.

After settling into camp life, I prepared for my first mission. The boss made me feel welcome and I finally started my new job – fuel convoys from Turkey. It was certainly an eye opener but I soon got into it.

Chapter 2

Convoy Missions

The following morning, I rolled out of bed and got dressed. It looked to be a great day: the sun was shining and we had a nice warm temperature with that lovely fresh morning smell you get. We had got up at 06.00 because we had a big convoy to escort down from Turkey. The convoy comprised fuel tankers headed for the US military.

Breakfast time was the normal shite: big queues with loads of hungry Yank soldiers. I had beans on toast with a mug of coffee and then got my gear ready. I was carrying an M16 assault rifle, an AK-47 Russian automatic rifle, plus a rucksack full of spare ammo. We always carried spare ammo – and lots of it – because we didn't know what we would encounter. It could be just one contact or even three or four on one trip, so we tried to prepare for every eventuality. I also loaded up with eighteen rounds of high-explosive 40mm grenades for my M203 grenade launcher, mounted under my M16. The reason for the AK-47, which I carried in the footwell of the truck, was that, because our contacts with the enemy happened so fast and were so intense, if you had a stoppage (basically if your main weapon jammed) you could just pick up your AK-47 and open up with that instead. Taking the time to try to clear your stoppage could cost you vital seconds during which you would be exposed and vulnerable. So it was a case of ditch the M16 and grab the AK-47.

At around 06.30 we went up to the ops room for a quick brief. This particular job today was fairly typical and was one we'd done loads of times before, so it was all pretty routine for most of the lads. However, because you learn on the job, nothing is ever routine in northern Iraq. That day, as it turned out, was going to be anything but routine. It was such a lovely morning that you could almost be mistaken for thinking you were somewhere else until the unmistakable sound of gunfire or bombs would jerk you back to reality. All the teams on this mission assembled on the main road leading up to the main gates of the camp. We checked our weapons – we were carrying more firepower than the American troops would. We had to. The Yanks could rely upon their armour, and bloody good it was as well, and they had air support, whereas we had to rely on firepower, aggression and speed, and we had plenty of all three. We just had Gurkhas and Fijians standing up in the backs of our trucks, almost in the open; the American troops had armoured gun turrets.

As we pulled up at the gate, the patrol leader gave the order to load and make ready all the weapons. We then did a comms check and switched on our bomb-jamming devices. We had one of these for every two vehicles, and on this job we had six vehicles. Two of our vehicles carried M240 heavy-duty machine guns on the back; two of our other vehicles had .50-cals; the remaining two vehicles had M19 automatic grenade launchers mounted. Each truck had four men inside, all carrying M16s and M249 squad automatic weapons. Some even, though only the Fijian guys mind you, carried M240 GPMGs. These M240s were big, heavy guns, so the Gurkhas couldn't individually handle them, but for the Fijians (who were huge guys) it was no problem. The more firepower we had, the better. We looked and were formidable and extremely effective. Due to the language barrier between the Gurkhas and the Fijians, we used to deploy them in separate patrols. Don't get me wrong, they all got on great, but it was just more efficient and safer for them to be in separate patrols to avoid any potential misunderstandings due to language difficulties.

Everyone and everything was now set. The engines of the Toyotas fired up, we did one last check and then we were off. As we got going I shouted, 'Heads up, lads!' as I always did to the guys in my truck. All the guys switched on as we gathered speed. The chains and wires on the gate were dropped and we flew out of it, tyres screeching as we slalomed through the concrete bollards. This tactic (the speed and swerving) was to try to avoid sniper fire. As soon as we departed, the guys started hard-targeting and the gunners on the back were spinning around checking out any likely sniper positions – this was where we started earning our money.

The task we had would probably seem pretty crazy to most people. First, we had to make it to the Turkish border, which was about an hour and a half away, at least. Hopefully, we'd get there in one piece, all the time dodging roadside bombs and sniper fire. Then we had to pick up and escort some one hundred fuel tankers through the most dangerous place in the world. This particular journey up to the north of Iraq went pretty smoothly, with no bombs or small-arms fire, which was pretty unusual, actually, as we normally encountered some kind of shit. As we got into the desert and were heading towards Turkey, everyone started to relax a bit. The area we were passing through was pretty open, with rolling hills and no cover for insurgents to hide in wait, so we were as safe as we could be. We went off-road and went into all-round defence. We decided to let the guys have a break and something to eat, so we stopped for a coffee and a snack, as this was just the beginning of what was to turn out to be one hell of a long day. All joking apart, you really did have to keep your energy levels up. If there was trouble, it could be hours and hours before you got into a safe enough place to stop and get something to eat.

In case you've never seen a Fijian soldier eat before, I've got to tell you it is one hell of a sight. The US army used to give us some of their rations for emergencies, in case we were ever caught out somewhere or had to go static for a few hours (sometimes we could actually end up stuck somewhere for hours and hours on end). Well, the Fijians would have a huge breakfast before leaving camp and then they would eat a load of the rations, which they followed with lunch and then dinner if they could. The Fijian guys I worked with were all massive, most of them stood 6 foot or well over and some of them had even played international-standard rugby for Fiji. Some of these guys had even played against England before!

After our feed and a bit of banter (the Fijians were all jokers and a real good crack – fantastic guys) we mounted up and headed out for the Turkish border. As we approached Kurdistan we all started to relax. The Kurds have it sewn up in Kurdistan. They man their own checkpoints, and if you're an Arab, you can't even take a crap up there without their knowing about it.

This place is where the US military, bodyguard teams and PMCs came to chill out and even do some shopping in the local markets. The markets were amazing, you could buy anything there – even AK-47s for as little as $100 on the black market. Everyone was so friendly and always seemed pleased to see you. There are some beautiful places in Kurdistan. A vast amount of the country is powered by hydro-electricity and there are some beautiful lakes up there, which are used to power the turbines.

As we weaved up and down these northern mountain roads on the way to the Turkish border, I had some big nostalgia trips, for these were the roads that I had used during the First Gulf War, when we were entering Iraq via the Turkey–Syria border; if we weren't dropped in by chopper we'd drive. I tried my best to remember exact routes and scanned my maps but it had been thirteen years since I'd been in these parts of the country.

We travelled along and at every checkpoint we came across we just went on through without stopping. Our teams didn't stop for anyone, no one except for the US military. Upon arrival at the border we were confronted with eighty fuel tankers and one of the tanker drivers taking a crap right there out in the open! These people have no shame! Our boss then went to do the paperwork that enabled us to proceed to carry out the protection for the convoy we were assigned to escort. This time, instead of the one hundred, it was going to be around eighty articulated fuel tankers (which was twenty fewer than we had been led to expect).

Now it doesn't take a rocket scientist to tell you that, if an insurgent were to fire a rocket or detonate a bomb near one of these things, you will have one hell of a bang and it would be blown to bits, and, if we were too close, probably some of us as well! Our job had just got a lot more interesting. Eighty tankers packed with highly flammable petroleum to be escorted and protected through probably one of the most dangerous places in the world. People thought we were fucking mad, and at that time we probably were. However, because of the geography of northern Iraq, the only routes past these hotspots meant we had to go right through the middle of them. Anyway, more often than not, the only decent routes were the main roads, which took you through the centre of these places.

We had a ruthless professional reputation that preceded us and we knew that, although it was fucking dangerous, we would get the job done. Most of the tanker drivers were Turkish, but there were quite a few Kurds as well. Upon inspection, we found that some of the tankers were in a shocking condition and, looking at them, we thought that there was no way they'd make it all the way to Baghdad without breaking down somewhere along the way. The convoy drivers and their bosses had their brief, which was basically this: don't fuck around; keep up and keep together; if you break down, you have only a few minutes to try to fix the thing; if you can't fix them quickly, you'll have to leave the tanker by the roadside and jump in with one of the other drivers – it's that or face certain capture by the insurgents. After a quick chin-wag with the leading guys we were off.

As we got closer and closer to Mosul (right up in the north of Iraq) the level of potential danger increased and everyone became a lot more focused, as this situation we were in was very, very serious. You have to make difficult decisions on your own sometimes and often right on the spot – how far to go and what risks to take, etc. You also have to accept the embarrassment of being wrong sometimes and the responsibility for any mistakes you make because in our situation you have nobody to hide behind – the buck stopped with us, the team leaders! You are always trying to second-guess the insurgents, since it's not only your life on the line, but you have the lives of your team and the tanker drivers lives in your hands, too. You learn how to read situations and you have to be disciplined to do this job. Most normal company employees are used to operating under strict rules and regulations. In Iraq there are none; you make your own rules and hope you've got it right. Most people go to work in a tie and jacket; we went to work in flak jackets and carrying guns – big guns.

As we got closer to town I flicked on the bomb-jamming equipment. The reason the bomb-jamming equipment wasn't left on all the time was that it often interfered with some of the communication equipment. As we got nearer, I tightened my hand on the pistol grip of my M16. I then popped a 40mm grenade into the launcher attached below and cocked it. It was time to earn our cash again. We had two vehicles at the front of the convoy, two more trucks travelling at the back and another two travelling up and down the length of the convoy. Everything was going according to plan so far, and then, out of the blue, a truck pulled over sharpish. One of our call signs stopped with it – it was inconveniently breaking down (apparently, an air leak in the brake system) and it couldn't go on; it was knackered. The driver was adamant he was staying with his lorry.

Now this was dodgy as fuck. If the insurgents were to

pass him they'd get his fuel and probably – no, make that
definitely – execute him, more than likely by lopping off his
head, though only after a good bit of torture! Our guys
heatedly explained this to him and he finally jumped into
another tanker and then we were off again. The convoy
hadn't stopped – we would never, ever stop, not for
anybody. The tanker that picked up the, now redundant,
driver just dropped to the back of the convoy. We couldn't
afford to stop; we had to keep the momentum.

As we were settling into our well-practised routine of
keeping these trucks as safe as we could, we came under
fire. Bang! Bang! Bang! in quick succession. Then more
rounds came down. They weren't that effective. The
insurgents were just having pot shots at the drivers of the
tankers, not us in the gun trucks. My team were frantically
trying to identify the source of the gunfire, but I was just
waiting for the insurgents to let rip with a bloody RPG,
which would be just our luck.

My gunner, in the back of the truck, was frantically
spinning around, itching to blow the crap out of the
arseholes shooting at us, but his discipline was great. He
could easily have just opened up at anything that moved.
However, by this time my gunner had been in Iraq for nearly
two years and he was a great shot, and if he had located the
fire point he would have had 'em big time. We thought it
was only going to be small-arms fire because, surely, if they
had an RPG they would have fired it by now. Looking
behind us, I saw a tanker break file and screech to a halt so

violently it almost jackknifed. We dropped back to see what had happened to it.

As soon as we pulled up I could hear the driver screaming. He'd been shot through the hand. It looked a bit messy and no doubt it hurt like hell, but it looked like he was going to be OK. I jumped up and dragged him out of the cab and told him to stop screaming like a baby; but, then again, if you've never been shot through the hand I don't suppose you know how painful it actually is. You could actually see straight through his hand (it brought to mind that scene in from the movie *From Dusk Till Dawn* when Quentin Tarantino's character, Richard Gecko, gets shot through the hand!).

Our medic wrapped a dressing around his wounded hand and taped it up tight with some electrical tape. We then bundled him into another tanker and we put our foot down to catch up with the rest of the convoy, which hadn't waited for us – that was our standard operating procedure, up to a point.

As we came to the outskirts of the town, my adrenalin was pumping and I kept my thumb on my safety catch. We all carried a different selection of weapons for a reason: it was because we were getting into unconventional situations and no one knew what we would need. Having to go up against all kinds of things that could be difficult, most of us carried the standard American M16s but a few of our guys carried the HKG3 (Heckler & Koch G3) because of its heavier calibre (7.62 mm) – it was a lot more effective at stopping vehicles that got too close. A 5.56mm round would bounce off an engine block sometimes but a 7.62mm would penetrate it and stop it dead (hopefully). A few of the veterans, who'd worked in Bosnia and Somalia and had been working as contractors for years, still favoured the AK-47, which I personally think was pretty inaccurate but was deadly effective and had a lot more stopping power. The 5.56mm round was brought into service years and years ago because it was so much lighter than the 7.62mm, and you could carry a lot more ammunition; so, although it was still quite capable of killing people, it couldn't quite hack taking out engine blocks. For this reason we needed the 7.62mm.

We came off the main road and started making steady progress through the town. The two vehicles that roamed up and down the convoy sped ahead and set up roadblocks. Nothing stopped us – nothing. We gave clear and precise warnings and had signs written in Arabic on the vehicles warning anyone to stay at least 20 metres away from us. If they came any closer, they'd become a target. If a vehicle came too close a few rounds were fired in front of it. If that didn't stop it, then we would shoot out the tyres. If it still came onto us, the engine was shot up, then the driver and, most likely, any passengers! We couldn't afford to mess about taking unnecessary risks in these situations. A lot of the time it was a case of kill or be killed. It was a simple fact that you couldn't let unfamiliar cars get too close.

If we did somehow manage to get stuck in traffic – some

big traffic jam through a town, for instance – we would all jump out and mingle between the Iraqi traffic. Even most of the insurgents didn't want to kill their own, so we always took cover in between the Iraqis. However, that said, the things we saw did make us wonder sometimes.

We were doing quite well so far on this convoy. We'd lost only two of the tankers out of the eighty we were escorting and we'd had only one minor contact and one minor injury. We tanked on through the town with everyone getting out of the way. Because of the way we'd handled previous firefights, with total aggression and a huge amount of returned fire, a lot of the insurgents knew we would unleash hell on them were we to come under attack. American intelligence (probably our CIA mates) had told us that most of the insurgents would rather take on the US military than us. We were now nicknamed 'the Black Death' by the insurgents. Apparently, this was down to the colour of the Fijians and Gurkhas' dark skin. On a typical run we would usually lose about 15 per cent of our tankers, mainly due to breakdowns but often enough due to IEDs and RPGs.

We had now, at this time, travelled into the thick of it with our convoy, right into the centre of Mosul, and were nearing our final destination: an American airbase on the outskirts of the city. This is where we would drop the tankers off and the Americans would take over. We were on our last hurdle and only just around the corner from the base. By this time it was around midday and everything, so far, had gone really smoothly; but, as we were to find out, we had worse to come, worse than we could possibly have imagined.

We slowly approached the turning to get onto the main road that led up to the airbase. We slalomed in and out of the, now familiar, concrete bollards until all of the tankers were safely inside. You could actually see the relief on the faces of most of the drivers. Once parked up in files of ten in the huge lorry and fuel park, most of the drivers got out of their cabs, unrolled their prayer mats, then knelt down and started praying, no doubt in thanks that they had arrived in one piece – this time. Once their prayers were finished, they all then got their pots of tea going – very sugary and sweet. The drivers, because they could be on the road for days at a time, had compartments built onto the sides of the lorries that contained little stoves, food, kettles, cups, tea and sugar, so they were basically self-sufficient on the road.

Now that the mission had been safely completed, our medic went over to the driver who had been shot through the hand. He was still whinging but our medic tended to him. Each of our patrols had a fully qualified paramedic who carried everything needed to stabilise a casualty – big time. Our medics were of the highest standard – they had to be. Most were either ex-soldiers who had done a paramedics course after the military, or were patrol medics in the armed forces, but they had to be military-trained as well and they also had to be able to fight. Indeed, when I had been in the mob I had been trained as a medic and had spent 16 weeks training in an NHS hospital. However, my skills were not required here. I did have the skills and knowledge to help in an emergency but I had other responsibilities in this job, which took precedence here.

Our medics certainly earned their money and they saved a lot of lives. They really were shit hot, of the highest standard. Once the injured Turkish driver was patched up I drove him to the American hospital on base. He'd had a good dose of morphine when he'd arrived on base and now he'd stopping whinging – which was a relief (the Turks whinge like hell when they are not even injured – that is normal for them – so you can imagine what they're like when they *are* hurt). He had been irritating me with his constant whinging – even after the morphine. This thought made me feel slightly ashamed but that was how I felt. He had, after all, had a big hole, the size of a plum, clean through his hand and, when I asked for a look at it, I could clearly see the ground through his hand, so maybe I was being a little harsh on him.

Once I'd dropped him off I drove back to pick up the rest of my team and, surprise, surprise, they were eating – tucking right into the emergency rations. We carried loads, so it was no problem, but, with those Fijian guys making up a large part of our team, it was just as well we did. But at least now our truck was faster and lighter.

After our feed and once we'd made sure all our big Fijian guys were happy, we refuelled our Toyotas at the Yanks' fuel point, checked the oil and water, and then prepared for our dash back across town and back to our base for a nice warm shower and some more scran. It was 17.30-ish now and soon it would be getting dark. This made it even more dodgy for us, as it was obviously far easier for the insurgents to attack us and get away with it at night.

All our vehicles lined up at the gate; we gave a wave at the American sentries then our drivers gunned the throttles. We tore out of the gate, then back onto the main road, hitting 70 m.p.h. as quickly as we could. Cars could see us coming and were trying to get out of the way as quickly as possible. The thing is, the insurgents can be extremely effective. If they want to get you they will try whatever they think will work, all different tactics. All you can do is react with disciplined professionalism, give them all you've got and, should you get hit, do as much damage limitation as possible. Then take them out. Period. If they know this they are more likely to go for an easier target, maybe some sectarian murder or something similar.

The way 90 per cent of attacks happened was that first there would be an improvised explosive device (IED), which could be anything from a dead dog packed with explosives on the side of the road to a similarly packed parked car. The insurgents had even started removing kerbstones on the side of the road, putting 105mm high explosive shells behind them and packing in nails, bits of metal (basically any sharp object that could maim or kill) and replacing them so that you couldn't tell they'd been tampered with. You must admit, it's pretty ingenious. Then, after the IEDs exploded, the insurgents would follow up the ambush with RPK machine guns and AK-47 assault rifles. Mayhem. So if you were caught in a blast you had to be on your toes – if you survived it, and a lot of our guys didn't – because the blast was so powerful. And that was normally just the *start* of an attack. The insurgents ran their operation like a military campaign, they would have people spotting for them on the edge of town, giving them exact locations of Coalition forces, so they knew to be at just the right place at the right time. This was the reason we drove so fast through town: our company's policy was that (hopefully), because we drove as fast as we did, by the time the insurgents had seen us and been able to trigger their device, we'd have already gone past it and they would miss us. This often worked, but sometimes they saw us coming too soon – as they often posted lookouts – and sometimes it didn't.

If we had to stop for any reason we would debus (get out of the vehicles) and get behind cover. If there were other local cars around, we would get in between them and crouch down. Even the insurgents were reluctant to kill their own, so you were pretty safe mingling in crowds. Once we were under attack and had identified our targets, we would try to blow the crap out of them, if possible. If it was in town our gunners were disciplined: we opened up only with M16s, M240s and M249s. If we'd opened up with the M19 grenade launcher or the .50-calibre we would have blown houses away and taken towns apart, but our guys were professionals and none of us wanted to harm innocent civilians – none of us.

I know some people will think it is wrong but we weren't arsed about taking prisoners. We were just looking after our own butts. If you don't agree with this philosophy I'd put this book down now. I was just looking out for my lads and comrades. It was a deterrent, one of the main reasons for the insurgency not to take us on. The insurgents would rather take on the US military than us because they knew that we were unable to take them prisoner. Not for one minute am I suggesting that we would ever have executed them, but they would be disarmed and maybe get a beating and then be told to fuck off. If we could hand them over to the Iraqi police we would always try to do that, but this was not always possible, as it would mean going static in a potentially hostile situation, which was something we would always try to avoid.

As we drove through towns we could hear gunshots a lot of the time, some far away, some close, some hitting us and our men. I could see scorch marks and craters everywhere where IEDs had gone off, and sometimes you couldn't help wincing when you were coming up to a position that was renowned for IEDs – but we always tried to avoid those locations if we could. Every time we came through towns, we tried to take a different route but, unfortunately, coming up to our camp there were only two roads and two entrances, so you were limited when it came to this point. As we approached our base camp on this occasion, the sentries gave us a wave and dropped the wires and chains, so we were able to charge on through. Once inside, we pulled over, all got out and unloaded and cleared our weapons, and then raised our left arms in the air to show we were clear, meaning that we had no round up the spout.

This may sound stupid and obvious, but it was vitally important, because nobody wants to have a stupid and completely avoidable accident on camp (someone getting accidentally shot) because some arsehole on your team forgot to clear his weapon properly. Mistakes can happen, people forget, so we had to implement seemingly obvious procedures. It is the same as being in the UK armed forces: you have procedures you have to follow even if you think they are idiotically obvious. Better safe than sorry. Even now, over ten years since I left the forces, I check and double-check everything – to the annoyance of some of those close to me.

Everyone, now being safe-ish inside the camp, started to relax and began chatting and having a bit of a stretch. Being stuck in one of those vehicles, with some of the lads carrying so much kit with them that you barely had room to move, could cramp you up a bit sometimes or at least make you a bit stiff, and on a really long or tense mission it could become a real problem. This problem was even worse if you were in the back with the Fijian guys. I love them to bits but, as they were so huge, they easily seemed to take up as much room as two Gurkhas.

Stretches over, the team leaders then went to the ops room for a quick debrief and to find out the next detail and missions. We never knew what we would be doing next or when we could be going out again. It could be 03.00 or maybe we would have the day off to do some training. You just never knew what was in store. It wasn't a job, it was an adventure – and a fucking dangerous one at that!

After the debrief our boss told us about an incident earlier that day. Eight Iraqi contractors had been in the thick of it and in a right mess, getting bombed and shot at. To put it simply, there had been a firefight between these Iraqi private contractors and the insurgents. After the firefight the Iraqi contractors were injured and were taken to an Iraqi hospital instead of a Coalition camp hospital, which was a big mistake. There is pretty much no way insurgents could gain access to a Coalition hospital on a camp, but in the middle of an Iraqi town this would be a piece of piss for them with unimaginable consequences. The insurgents had then broken into the hospital and killed and decapitated the contractors.

The Yanks had picked up the bodies and heads and brought them back and put them in a small tent right outside our office (I know I keep calling the American troops 'Yanks' but 90 per cent are a great bunch and I've worked with them on many occasions, so no offence is intended). Sure enough, after a gander inside the tent we could see that there were actually eight bodies in body bags with their heads lopped clean off. Later we had the grisly task of moving them.

As we approached the tent, later that day, I was feeling a bit uneasy and I thought that, unless you were a serial killer, this was going to be quite unnerving. I wouldn't say I was scared, just really didn't want to see them. I haven't got a morbid streak (which is unfortunate, being a mercenary and ex-Marine). I'd rather be having a laugh outside with the lads. As a soldier you don't have that choice, but as a mercenary, or contractor, you do.

I remembered the aftermath of the First Gulf War when I was a young Royal Marine Commando twenty years old, having to clear up some real nasty shit, so I wasn't looking forward to this. It made the body bags feel weird to move with the heads rolling around inside. The heads eventually stopped rolling around and fell down to about the arse area, so it felt as if we were dragging their heads along the ground when we were actually carrying them. I had heard once somewhere that a head can weigh up to 2 stones and I had never believed it, but, after actually trying to pick one up by the hair (as I'd seen in so many movies), I realised that this is impossible: they're just too heavy and you have to pick them as you would a water melon – not a nice thing. It was pretty grim, but someone had to do it. In situations this grim, you sometimes get the giggles. Don't know if it's because it's so horrible or just the way your brain copes with it. But I decided I wasn't going to lose my head over it! Pardon the sorry pun, but picking up heads was something I'd never done before; in fact it was way outside any experience I'd ever had, thank fuck!

After doing the body thing I wasn't feeling that hungry and I considered skipping dinner and just going back to my accommodation, but I knew that I had to eat because the next day would be another long one and who knew what would happen? I went for a shower and scrubbed myself clean for ages, but I couldn't seem to get rid of that death smell. It felt as if I had absorbed it into my very pores. Once my skin was nearly raw I stopped scrubbing and just stood under the spray with my face turned upwards, letting the water wash over my head. I wanted to stay there but I knew I couldn't.

I got out and dried off, changed and made my way to the chow tent. I queued up and got my food and joined a couple of the guys, but nobody was feeling very talkative – we ate in silence. After scran, I went down to the gym to push some weights – I definitely needed another shower after that session. The gym was situated inside one of Saddam's presidential buildings. Being a US military gym, it had every bit of equipment you could imagine. American logistics are second to none when it comes to warfare, and they really have their shit together when it comes to looking after their troops. After a good training session, I wanted to call home. On camp we were given a satellite phone and a mobile phone each. The reception on the mobile phone was excellent and incredibly cheap, cheaper than ringing a mobile phone in the UK, actually! It worked out at about 20p a minute.

To start off, when I rang home to speak to my parents and sister in York, I'd tell them I was in some foreign country working on oil rigs, but a careless phone call from a mate – checking I was OK because he hadn't heard from me for a while (he knew where I was) – soon put a stop to that. My mum shat a brick. She burst into tears and begged me to come home. I said that I had an internal job at the airport that was really safe. She eventually swallowed it but I carried on lying about the location. My old man never asked me any questions. He was used to my doing dangerous work in fucked-up countries.

After the gym and my shower, I went back to my hooch – my accommodation – and started cleaning my kit and weapons. It was midsummer and really hot, so, once my weapons were as clean as it was really possible to get them, a few of the lads and I sat outside our huts and had a couple of cold beers.

The US military weren't allowed to drink, so we became very popular by giving them the occasional beer. Because we were officially civilians, we could drink. This had been a long day and we'd had a grisly task to perform, but our team had sustained no losses or injuries – so I guess that meant it was overall a good one. How can you say what is a good day? Nobody from our company had even been injured but eight guys from another security company doing, probably, the same job as we were doing had died. But we had far better backup; those poor men had none whatsoever. Poor souls!

After a couple of tins I went and got my head down. Next morning I reported for duty at 08.00 and we had a day of weapons training and vehicle drills. Nothing special, just a typical day around camp.

It's a very strange feeling when you look back on it. I've never slept so well or peacefully in my life as I did in Iraq. You are so removed from the rest of the world and I think because you use up a lot of adrenalin you end up being shattered and eventually get used to the dull thud of explosions and gunfire in the distance. Your body and mind adapt to the tone and noise and rhythms. If it's in the distance you sleep; if it comes close you jump instantly awake.

Convoy missions were our main task but each one was different. We had to take the rough with the smooth. Some went well and were almost easy; some were risky and violent and truly very distressing. After all, when you lose a colleague it's never nice.

Chapter 3

Big Contact

We'd been taking and getting quite a few casualties driving through all of these dangerous villages that were strongly occupied by insurgents. I think we'd had more of our guys killed on this northern mission than any other security company working in Iraq at that time. This was purely down to the intensity of the fighting up here, not down to the guys not knowing what they were doing or a lack of professionalism.

There were a lot of no-go areas for most of the private military companies in the north. However, we were often asked to actually go through some of these areas, which was always dodgy as hell. We could normally handle it because our guys were good and we had some awesome firepower. The Americans gave us pretty much whatever we wanted. Sometimes we just had to escort things and vehicles through and other times we were just asked to assess the threat level in the area for the US military. None of it, however, was a walk in the park. Far from it. There was danger lurking around every corner.

Two weeks before I arrived up in the north to start my new job, disaster struck. One of the teams – in fact the whole patrol – were approaching Mosul. Nothing out of the ordinary there for the team – just another run-of-the-mill trip. Everything had seemed normal – well, as normal as it's possible to get in the north. You quite often got the odd opportunist insurgent shooting at you, but unless you got hit by an IED you'd probably survive it with most of our casualties just suffering minor injuries. This day turned out to be a bad one for that particular team.

The insurgents had obviously been waiting for an American patrol to come through this particular area and were well prepared for them. When that didn't happen they just waited to pick another target – which that day was one of our patrols! The Yanks were probably avoiding the area after getting intelligence from their spooks, who then warned their own troops. However, that sort of intelligence rarely filtered down to us, so we often had no way of knowing when an attack was due or where it might come from. That was, indeed, the case for our company's patrol that day. I shall say *our* and *us* from now on, even though I was not personally present during this contact.

On this particular day, there were dozens of insurgents lying in wait for the guys. They were all armed to the teeth and they had planted quite a few IEDs all over the place (on this occasion they were lots of car bombs). As our teams came up the street, all the locals disappeared (which is always an indication that there's going to be trouble). Then – *boom*! The first IED went off at the beginning of the road, taking out our lead vehicle. The insurgents then started firing their AK-47s and RPKs from side streets, rooftops, windows, everywhere – you name it, they were there. Gunfire was hitting our guys from all directions, then – *boom* again! Another IED, another car bomb, then more firing.

Apparently, by this time, the teams could hardly even drive and make it up the road because of all the rubble and destruction. Our team was getting the shit kicked out of them and it was pure carnage. Our patrol then retaliated, firing back and ended up killing quite a few insurgents. They opened up with everything they had. This was a right mess. There was nothing the lads could do; they were in a right pickle.

Any civilian approaching was also getting injured or even killed for fear of being an insurgent who might have been about to chuck a grenade. Our guys had reasoned that any innocent civilians would take cover and not try to walk through the middle of a huge firefight. In fact, as the street had been so quiet, as if the locals had known what was about to go down, there hadn't been that many people about, although there were young men throwing things – rocks, grenades and so forth – at the guys. So any person walking out and about or throwing stuff either had a death wish or, more likely, was an insurgent. The situation was extremely bad and had deteriorated rapidly.

After eventually getting out of the kill zone, one of the trucks was fucked – blown tyres, shrapnel holes everywhere – and, worst of all, two of their Fijian comrades were dead after the initial IED. Also, one of the ex-SAS guys, who had been riding in the lead vehicle, had been shot in the head by a suspected ricochet. The Gurkha who was driving the truck carrying the ex-SAS guy must have had balls as big as an elephant because, after Justin (as I will call him) was hit in the head, he was, apparently, still alive. This brave little Gurkha had broken away from the main convoy and then he'd driven through Mosul, totally on his own, with no backup – leaving his convoy behind. Justin's injuries were so severe that the Gurkha knew that he had to get him to a hospital as soon as possible – he had been in an obviously critical condition with this very bad head injury. As he sped through town he was fired upon repeatedly, but he wouldn't and didn't stop.

As the Gurkha had approached the gates of the American camp, the sentries on duty saw all the bullet holes and got the medics on standby. They'd also been made aware of the contact report, so they knew of the situation. This brave little Gurkha drove his arse off to get Justin to hospital as soon and as fast as possible, but it was all in vain: Justin was dead on arrival. His head injuries were too severe. So that had been the situation: quite a few (thirty-two) insurgents lay dead and three of our guys were dead. Not good, not good at all. It had been one hell of a firefight and one hell of a mess.

Pete Mercer

Soon after the two Fijians had arrived at the same American base for medical treatment, one guy was clearly dead on arrival but, amazingly, one was still alive – just. Unfortunately, as they were lifting him out of the back of the truck, he passed away. He'd been ripped apart by one of the car bombs and most of his legs were missing, but I was told he had been a hulk of a guy and the medics had said it was a miracle that he had survived long enough to get back to camp with the extent and severity of his wounds. Everyone had shed a tear for their colleagues.

Because quite a few civilians in the town had been killed in the crossfire, the US military wanted an explanation for what had happened. However, because we were contractors, we didn't have to fill out contact reports. Officially, as civilians, an oral explanation would be acceptable for them. It was a nightmare of a day for our guys and, every time that kind of shit happens (someone getting injured or killed), it bangs it home to everyone how fucking dangerous that place is.

After clearing out Justin's locker, one of our guys had resigned and some of the other guys had seriously thought about it. Apparently, seeing Justin's pictures of his wife and kids banged it home to this guy how quickly things could go bad for anybody working here and he must have thought of his own family and said, Fuck it! It's not worth earning all this money if you're not going to be around to spend it with your family. It made more than a few of our guys question whether they should be out there at all.

Situations like that really made everybody think about their own mortality.

It was one of the first things I was told when I first arrived, however. I was single and I must admit that I had a bit of a 'don't give a fuck' attitude at the time. Things weren't good at home and I just wanted to earn some good money. Getting up there (to Mosul) had been traumatic enough, and then you get some arsehole giving you war stories and trying to scare the shit out of you. Not a tactic I'd ever employ, but it happened a lot.

As I'd put myself up for this job I fully realised that the mess I was in now was entirely of my own doing. Hell, I'd even badgered the boss in Baghdad to send me up here. The contacts we were encountering up here were very intense and you had to have your wits about you all the time. As I said, on most of our missions we were losing men at quite an alarming rate and this wasn't including the major and minor injuries that we sustained on a regular basis.

So here I was with a bunch of guys who were constantly getting their arses shot off but, on the bright side, they were great to work for and with. This was certainly the craziest job I'd ever undertaken. Danger was everywhere.

Chapter 4

Tal Afar

The Gurkhas never ceased to amaze me. We had a mixed bunch. There were the British-trained and the Pakistani-trained Gurkhas, but apart from their training differences they had one thing in common: their unwavering loyalty. These guys would often be involved in very nasty contacts, losing comrades sometimes on a daily basis. Even when one or more of them were maimed or killed and you told them the next detail, or job, was at, say, 04.00 the next day, they would all be there, ready and raring to go. No moaning, no complaints – just ready. These little guys were fearsome. What some of them lacked in their training they made up for in their courage. You could always train them in tactics but you could never give them balls.

I woke up that morning and did my normal routine of shaving and showering and going for a good breakfast, after which, as I walked back to the accommodation, I saw Triple Canopy drive past. They must have had a VIP with them, because in front and behind the armoured SUV that they were escorting they had their armoured Hummers with .50-cals on the turrets. These guys used to take care of all the American VIPs (senators, ex-presidents and what have you) who came to visit. They were a friendly bunch and we all got on well, but we didn't discuss many missions between companies that much.

Once up at the ops room I was told we would be taking a route through Tal Afar for this mission. This wasn't my normal patrol route, but I'd asked to go because this was a route I'd never taken before. I'd been in this job only a few months, and it's advantageous to know as many routes around the north as possible, because you never knew what diversions or evasive routes you might have to take if you hit bad trouble. As my own personal patrol was doing weapons training that day, it would be no problem for me to miss it. The other patrol commanders could do the instruction.

After the Gurkhas had finished their breakfast they started to get the trucks ready, which always put a smile on my face. The Fijians, when they loaded their trucks, would just pass the heavy weapons up to one another as if they were toy guns. This was because of their huge size and strength. The Gurkhas, however, had to get five or six of themselves around the .50-cals to get them up. Another funny thing was the winter Gore-Tex jackets they were all issued with: they came in only two sizes and those were large and extra large. Even the extra-large jackets used to look tight on some of the Fijians, but the large jackets would swamp some of the Gurkhas, making them look as if they were wearing trench coats. The gunners on the back of the Hiluxes had to be kept warm, though, because the temperature was now very low. Plus, with the wind-chill factor, they sometimes had ice on them after a particularly long and cold run. We tried to incorporate more stops on our missions to keep them warm and make them more comfortable, without compromising our security, if it was possible. Neither the Gurkhas nor the Fijians ever moaned, though. They were professionals and hard as nails. I had a lot of respect for these men.

As contractors working in northern Iraq, sometimes we walked a fine line between being security personnel and mercenaries. To look at us and the weapons we carried and our tactics, you'd think we were some kind of paramilitaries. You can argue the toss all day: contractor, private military or mercenary. All I know is that I got paid a lot of money to look after and protect people and property. If trouble ever found us, so be it! We would deal with it using all the resources available to us – and we had a lot. We wouldn't look for trouble, far from it. It was the team leader's job in each of our patrols to avoid it at all costs, but we would not shy away from it, either. In the job we were doing people die; it's part of the job. We were all there by choice and were there for the dosh. If you don't agree or don't want to do it, you go home. Period.

On this particular day it wasn't much different from any other, as always the heavy weapons were fitted to the vehicles and all the spare ammo was loaded into the back along with, if you couldn't guess, boxes and boxes of MREs (the American emergency food rations). It wasn't unknown for us to sometimes get through 3,000–4,000 rounds in a large contact, our main tactic when being hit was to put down a large amount of fire and get the fuck out of the area as fast as possible. Being fully financed by the US Government, we had no shortage of weaponry and ammunition. We went through our usual routine of checking and double-checking our radios, weapons, bomb-jamming equipment, sat-nav and other communication means. We then went through the IA (immediate-action) drills quickly. These were mainly generic, but, for the mission we were now tasked with, we would be travelling through an insurgent stronghold so we really had to hammer it home to the lads to be on their toes, as this was going to be fucking dangerous, more dangerous than Mosul.

Tal Afar is a city in northwestern Iraq in the Ninawa Governorate, located approximately 30 miles west of Mosul and 120 miles northwest of Kirkuk. While no official census data exists, the city has been assessed as having a population of approximately 220,000 people, nearly all of whom are Iraqi Turkmen. The population's religious affiliation is split roughly in halves, between Sunni Muslims and Shia Muslims. While most residents do speak Arabic, a dialect of Turkish is also used almost universally throughout the city.

After the US invasion of Iraq in 2003, insurgents used Tal Afar as a staging point for most of their attacks. In September 2004, American forces stormed in and defeated the insurgents and left roughly six-hundred troops in the city, and this was the time we were tasked to travel through this stronghold. This was not good. Later, however, the Iraqi authorities lost control over the city and in May 2005 the insurgents began taking over again.

Military operations in June 2005 did not quell the violence. Final offensive operations involving eight-thousand Iraqi and US troops were launched in September 2005. They tried, and successfully used, a new strategy of clearing, holding and building in the areas that they had purged of insurgents. An ambitious reconstruction effort was implemented. Most of the sewers had to be replaced after the attacks and this was done within a matter of weeks. Tal Afar has also been the scene of sectarian violence between the Shi'ite and Sunni Muslims. In May 2005 clashes broke out between the two groups. In March 2006 President George W Bush highlighted Tal Afar as a success story, but I personally feel that this was a bit premature, as the fighting continues to this day with some ferocity. On 27 March 2007 a truck bomb exploded, killing 152 people and injuring a further 347.

However, for us in 2004, there was going to be a lot of resistance, but I'll tell the whole story, to give you an idea of how bad it actually was. We were to be travelling through this place at the height of its violence. With a total area of approximately 10 square miles there were a lot of places from which we could get ambushed, bombed or shot at. At the brief before going out on patrol, we gave the lads a heads-up and told them that this was going to be a dangerous one. But nothing fazed these guys.

As we left the gate as normal, I prepared the guys, explaining that it was likely we would have a contact of some sort today, be it a major one or minor. I just knew it was going to come at some point. We knew this was going to be a bit dodgy. You can't expect to breeze through an insurgent stronghold without an incident of some kind. We'd studied the map and it was the only route we could travel to get to where we were going. On this particular job, we had to escort one of the American special-ops guys to the other end of the town and, hopefully, get him and us there in one piece. This job we were doing was outrageous and hard to take in sometimes, but I would be a liar if I said I wasn't enjoying it a little bit.

We burst out of the gate in our typical style – fast and aggressive – and then cleared the chains, so now we were definitely on our way. I was slightly apprehensive about this mission but excited nevertheless. I always worried about the guys in my team. They were like brothers to me now and I was always trying to make sure they were OK. Being responsible for the lives of four guys always adds pressure and a certain level of stress in situations like these. If or when any of our guys were killed or badly injured, you always tormented yourself with thoughts of how you could have done things differently – hindsight always being 20–20.

As we started to travel through Mosul, we heard the occasional gunfire; we always did, but it was nothing we weren't used to. We travelled past the familiar places on our new mission to Tal Afar. Noticeably, one of them was the giant mosque that the US government were paying to be built to try to pacify the local community. Unfortunately for us and the US troops, it was becoming popular with insurgent snipers: because of the height of the building, it had great vantage points for them. In situations like these, where you were going into the unknown, you had to be spontaneous and improvisational. A lot of the time there was no bloodshed, but the energy was often ugly and violent. You can often sense bad vibes: sometimes it's like the calm before the storm; sometimes it's the look in people's eyes. It can be many things, but you know – you sense it. Gut instinct, if you like.

We sped across this dangerous city and we were soon clearing the outskirts of Mosul when I saw two white camels tethered at the side of the road; I couldn't believe my eyes, this place was mad. We sped along into the desert and, as we'd now cleared Mosul, everyone started to chill a bit. I radioed 'Patrol clear' as we cleared the town. 'Roger. Out,' came the reply from the patrol commander. I was still tail-end Charlie at this point. We were all a bit more relaxed now. The only threat to us was from IEDs, and there wasn't much you could do about those except keep your eyes peeled and look for something that could contain one. But, as we've seen, the insurgents would hide them in the most ingenious places. Most of the time you knew one was there only when it went off, and then it was too late – you were fucked.

When we could no longer see civilisation, we pulled over into a bit of cover and went into all-round defence (all of our tail gunners facing outwards) so the guys could have a piss stop and, you guessed it, some elevenses. They'd gone a couple of hours now with no food and they needed topping up! We got the flasks out. We tried never to use the same place to stop at twice within, say, a month to prevent the insurgents from getting familiar with our movements and planting booby traps or mines.

The temperature was coming up a bit now and the sun was warming the desert by a few degrees. After some coffee and some American MRE (meal, ready-to-eat) rations, we loaded up and carried on. Everyone was now feeling recharged and raring to go. I was mentally going through my contact drills and did a few radio checks with the other call signs. I reiterated to the lads that something would probably happen (major or minor I couldn't say; after all, we weren't fortune tellers). They all now had their serious heads on – this was almost coming up to show time.

We were now about 5 kilometres away from Tal Afar and could clearly see the outskirts of the city. Also, we had started to drive past some basic little huts by the sides of the road, complete with wild dogs barking and running out at us. This was new territory to us and we didn't really know what to expect, so, a few kilometres later, before we got to this hellhole, we pulled over and had a pow-wow. There wasn't much to plan for. The main reason we'd stopped was to make sure everyone was ready for a bad firefight. Minutes later we were tearing off again into the unknown. We were averaging about 60 m.p.h. and we'd got our spacing spot on. Everyone was covering his arc of fire. I put my thumb on the safety catch of my M16 and popped a 40mm grenade into the breach of my M203 grenade launcher.

We were now approaching the edge of the city and my concentration was honed. Everyone started hard-targeting (moving the weapon in the direction you are looking), scanning for likely ambush positions. The main road coming into town was actually really quiet. As our convoy approached we were fired upon from quite a distance – nothing serious as of yet, but we couldn't afford to take any chances. Any way you looked at it, it was incoming fire and a 7.62mm round can be effective up to 1,600 metres. That's not too far off a mile. Even if they couldn't see us properly and they just sprayed a burst of automatic gunfire in our direction, there was a very real chance that a stray round could hit one of us.

There were wadis (valleys or dry river beds) either side of the road which we could drive the vehicles into, if needs be, and turn around if we had to, or take cover in if things were to get too serious. The insurgents' fire at this time wasn't

effective, though, and we weren't 100 per cent sure it was
even aimed at us, as there were American patrols in the area
and they (the insurgents) could be having a pop at the Yanks
rather than at us. But it made it more difficult for us to be
sure if we were the targets, because we couldn't identify
where the insurgents' fire was coming from. We carried on
regardless. In the next moment the vehicle in front of us
swerved. Hmm, this was not at all normal.

It was etched on my consciousness how badly and rapidly
situations could deteriorate in Iraq. My worst fear of all was
capture, for this would surely mean days or weeks of
horrific torture followed, almost certainly, by beheading. I'd
rather top myself. For any contractor working in Iraq this
would be the absolute worst-case scenario and it was just
totally unthinkable.

The front vehicle came to a stop on the side of the road.
The front right-hand-side wheel and tyre had been shot out.
We had a choice: torch and blow up the vehicle and leave it
for dead, or assess how effective the insurgent attack was
and then stay and fix the tyre. We were quite a way from the
enemy fire point, which we'd assessed was a block of flats
to our right (a good 1,000 metres away). We didn't want to
let rip with the M19 grenade launcher or the .50-cal and
take the complex totally out because, knowing the
insurgents, that block of flats could be populated by women
and children and we always did all we could to avoid
collateral damage. Killing innocent civilians was not in our
code. While we were deciding what to do for the best, the

Gurkhas, cool as cucumbers, just calmly got out of the truck
and started changing the wheel. One Gurkha had the jack
and another had the wheel brace and they carried on as if
they didn't have a care in the world. We started putting
down covering fire for them. Mad little fuckers!

We were pretty much pinned down, though, and there
was no way we would be able to get through this town
safely; and, as we got closer, the firing would almost
certainly become more intense. We were in trouble. Best
thing we could hope to achieve was to fix the wheel, then
turn around to get the fuck out of Dodge. I was shouting to
the Gurkhas to keep their heads down, but they didn't seem
to care. They'd been through a lot of firefights in Iraq and a
lot of them were religious and believed in fate and karma:
what will be will be. They didn't seem scared of death. I just
thought they were little nutters but we were all on the same
page when it came to the tasks and missions we were given
– we all just wanted to get out of there in one piece. These
guys were priceless.

The road right next to where the mad Gurkhas were
changing the wheel was now littered with hundreds of
empty bullet cases and I did my best to control the rate
of fire from our guys. When you're not taking casualties
and you've got the upper hand and superior firepower,
you can find these situations quite exhilarating. My
senses were sharp but, in the back of my mind, I was
always thinking that to try to take the fight to the
insurgents was suicide.

It could easily have been a come-on – a trap. Insurgents had used this tactic very usefully and cleverly with American troops in the past. The insurgents would start off with a very small force, and then often retreat. The Yanks would then do a follow-up, and then there would be loads of insurgents waiting in ambush with explosives and all kinds of ordnance to take them out. This was certainly one situation we would never purposely get into. Our job was simple: get from A to B with as little hassle as possible. At the end of the day, all we wanted was to get home in one piece. Although I did wonder about one or two of the guys!

The wheel on the Hilux was now done and there was no more damage to the vehicle. It was now decided to do a fighting withdrawal and come back the way we'd come. Tal Afar seemed too fucking risky to go through at this time. If the insurgents in the meantime had managed to circle us we would then be in the desert and could let rip with everything we had: M19s, M203s, M240s, M249s and .50-cals. I had a strong feeling the insurgents also knew this and, as I said before, they're not stupid. It was an acceptable risk for us to attempt; plus, we had little or no choice: to try to pass their fire position was suicide, because they were fortified and well armed. We were in a no-win situation.

As we mounted up and prepared to get out of the area, we put down more suppressing fire on the flats, when an American Stryker patrol showed up and we all took cover behind these huge armoured vehicles. The Stryker commander, a captain, jumped down. 'You guys OK? We heard a lot of shooting so we came to investigate. You guys need a hand?' We explained in detail about our predicament. After discussing our options the American captain said, 'Why don't I just fire some missiles at that goddamned block of flats, then you can drive right on through?' We explained about not wanting to injure or kill civilians and our aim to minimise collateral damage. He told us that the apartments were still under construction and no one lived there. The insurgents used them quite frequently to ambush American troops. I think he just wanted an excuse to flatten them. That was all the information we needed. 'Flatten the fuckers,' our boss said. The Yank smiled and jumped back into his big fuck-off machine of destruction and gave the order.

We all watched with anticipation as the three Strykers trundled off down the main road until they were level with the apartments. We could all hear the AK-47 rounds, fired by the insurgents, just bouncing off their armour. That was fucking ace! The twats in the flats were going to get one hell of a shock. You could see the missiles' homing system targeting the flats, and then, in an instant, there were two whooshes and we followed the trail of smoke from the missiles hurtling towards the apartments. These missiles were awesome and in a split second three floors of the block were no longer there – just dust and rubble. Lo and behold – no more incoming firing! Fucking excellent!

It was pure poetry in motion. Killing another human being is not something to relish, but the fact was that these insurgents were trying and doing their damnedest to send us to a better place (or worse) – that made them fair game. I laughed my head off. I definitely have my own set of morals.

The apartments were no more – just dust. Our wheel was fixed and there were not so many insurgents left – none who could fight anyway. Life was peachy. Now that the Yanks had done our dirty work for us, there was pretty much no resistance left. We were all on a bit of a buzz now and all of us were laughing our heads off at what a bizarre situation we'd just been part of.

It was lovely to see the guys smile. They were always in the thick of it and, although they were tough bastards, a bit of relief never came amiss. Now this was something that could have come right out of a movie (a crap one, admittedly) – little guys fixing a wheel while under quite intense enemy fire. Even some of the hardened, veteran ex-SAS/SBS found it hysterical. It added a whole giggle factor to the totally fucked-up situation we had just survived; but, on the other hand, we were all deadly serious – we had to be.

In hindsight we should have just blown the damaged Toyota to pieces, left it for dead and carried on; but, as I said, the energy in the area was ugly and violent. However, there was no bloodshed this time apart from the bad guys. When those missiles hit they wouldn't have known anything about it. They would have just been taken out. There would have been nothing left.

In situations like this you have to think on your feet and, as I've said, at the end of the day I was responsible for four of these brave little fuckers in my truck. If one of them had died or been maimed . . . . Well, does anyone know how to write in Nepalese to one of their loved ones to say sorry? Because I fucking don't. The British forces in these war zones have to be in these danger areas. I have the utmost admiration for these people and, time and time again, they are bound by duty to be there getting their arses shot off, but we, as private contractors, were are all there by choice. Sometimes not the smartest thing to do.

Now, back to those wheel-changing nutters. After taking stock of our tactical miscalculation (fuck-up, basically) we decided to get the hell out of Dodge ASAP and, because of the kind support of the Yanks, we had little resistance. We screeched off with the Gurkhas. The one driving us in our vehicle was using a booster cushion. I'm not kidding you, this guy was tiny, only about 5-foot-nothing, but he had balls as big as an elephant. Because of the intensity of the situation, he ended up driving like Lewis Hamilton, so we were now going through Tal Afar pretty fast. This little Gurkha could drive like the wind (I was, personally, bricking it) even if he could hardly touch the pedals.

Tal Afar was truly mental. I've never been through such a place. The local people seemed to wear vacant expressions on their faces, but as there was so much fighting in the city – in fact, there seemed to be fighting everywhere – I guess they were just numb to their circumstances. We all knew we just needed to get out of there, and fast, before things got any worse.

We flew through Tal Afar and we were soon on the outskirts of the city. As we were driving so fast, we unfortunately hit a mother dog; she was killed instantly but the puppy with her wasn't. Because of the lower risk in the area we were now in, and because we were a bunch of soft bastards, we stopped and picked up the puppy and put her in the back of the truck. We decided to keep her, and we named her Kasper (after a good friend of mine). In the war zone it is definitely true that soldiers or mercenaries can be some of the softest bastards you will ever meet when it comes to animals and not humans. So now we had ourselves a pet.

I'm not going to lie to you and say Iraq, especially Fallujah, Mosul and Tal Afar, are out-and-out firefights every day, but it could be vicious and our personnel casualty rate was 47 per cent overall. Obviously, this was nearly half of our guys. We were losing an average of one or two guys a month through death or serious injury. This was far from our lack of professionalism; rather it was down to our being in the worst hotspot in Iraq. It made me think sometimes that I should have got a job in Tesco! All joking aside, the soldiering side of you loves it, but the family-man side (and your conscience) can sometimes deplore it.

As we ploughed through and out of Tal Afar we could see the American forces walking behind their armoured vehicles while on patrol, especially on the outskirts of town. You couldn't blame them (if we had armour-plated vehicles we would definitely have done the same). We just fired straight past them at breakneck speed with a quick wave as a good-luck gesture. This was bandit country after all. They all thought we were crazy fuckers for having no doors on and hardly any armour. I was beginning to think that they were right.

As we got through this broken, tattered city it was obvious these people were in a mess. Something was wrong. The hearts-and-minds strategies weren't working. When the US military accused the British forces in Basra of losing the battle for hearts and minds, I personally was a little bit disgusted. The British are very good at hearts and minds – as good as the Americans, I believe. Hearts and minds can win wars. I apologise to any Americans reading this, but don't take it personally. It's just my personal view – take it or leave it.

Tal Afar is a crazy place – an insurgent stronghold. I wouldn't call it fun because this was still going to be a tough escape – basically trying to get out of this place in one piece. It was going to be a major escape. The American forces at the time were having a pretty hard time trying to keep control of the place. For everyone who works in Iraq who is of white or European origin, their worst fear is capture. If you were unlucky enough to get caught the consequences are unimaginable: days, weeks or possibly even months of torture. And I've already spelled out the likely consequences of that: certain beheading, after which I've personally had to pick up the pieces. I've read quite a bit of the Koran and know that the people who do these atrocities are hypocrites. They don't believe in good or bad: they believe in their way or no way. I've some very good Muslim friends and they feel the same as me about this.

Once we'd hit the outskirts of Tal Afar with our new pet tied on the back of one of the trucks, we started to relax a bit, when, to our slight shock and surprise, we encountered a big burst of automatic gunfire. This place never let up! We couldn't pinpoint where it came from, just that it was from our right. A stray round then winged one of the Gurkha gunners, who was on the back of one of the trucks. We just ploughed on, though – we had to. To stop would have been suicide.

I've worked for unprofessional companies with idiots working for them out in Iraq. They would probably have just started blasting away at anything that moved in a situation like the one we were now in. This is totally counterproductive, doing more harm than good. As you travelled through towns like these, some of the locals would often actually warn you of imminent danger and guide you away from what would almost certainly end up with the demise of some of your team in some sort of explosion or ambush. So it is always the smart option to keep some or as many locals on your side as possible.

This can also be a double-edged sword, though, as they could quite as easily be leading you into some sort of a trap.

You have to make a rapid risk assessment on the spot, but a good rule of thumb is not to go down any narrow streets that could end up in any unfamiliar potential cut-off points. If you're on one of the main routes you can almost take it as gospel that there is going to be some sort of device that's going to do you some real harm: take out, kill or maim your patrol. This was part and parcel of the job; there wasn't a lot you could do about it.

As we were getting to the relatively safe areas, adrenalin was now slowing down, so we stopped to assess and stabilise the injured Gurkha (poor little fucker). His injuries weren't life-threatening and our medic did a fantastic job of patching him up. What had happened was that he'd had one round go through the right shoulder just below the clavicle – serious but he'd get to go home with a lot more medical insurance money in his pocket than he would have earned the whole of that year in Iraq, plus some great scars to show the girls when he arrived back in Nepal!

Everyone was now buzzing from the contact we'd just gone through – and it is a massive, massive buzz – probably from the amount of fire being put down from the Iraqi insurgents. I think that, after this one, we sent quite a few of the insurgents off to paradise and I think the Yanks would definitely have to stump up for a new apartment building! All my company would have to fork out for would be a new wheel. With all of this gung-ho shit, you'd think you would want to be getting to a safe place as soon as possible, but I tell you what sometimes: do you fuck! 'Bring it on' was the case sometimes. The smell of cordite does get you going and you feel alive and invincible at times. Of course, it's pure testosterone and adrenalin kicking in most of the time. Difficult to explain to some people, perhaps.

As we'd now cleared the worst of it all, we were still on edge a bit, but our little colleague was fine. We'd had no further casualties so far and things were looking good. However, as we approached Mosul we had a bit of a scare – nothing serious but quite spectacular. While we'd been away, the insurgents had launched a combined attack on the Yanks. This attack had involved RPGs, mortars and gunfire. The Yanks in turn had called in a huge airstrike on them; this was truly awesome. We had to go firm, get defensive immediately, and then we settled back to watch the fireworks. To watch these fighter planes (F-16s) drop from the skies along with Apache attack helicopters sending guided missiles into houses is something awesome and was certainly better than Guy Fawkes Night. Our new puppy was completely oblivious to all of this and slept right on through it!

After witnessing these dramatic airstrikes and with, no doubt, an untold amount of dead or wounded insurgents, altogether we'd had quite a busy day trying to get through what must be one of the toughest cities in Iraq. We hadn't delivered our package or completed the mission, but we'd had no losses. Of course, one of the guys had sustained a gunshot wound and we'd had a blown tyre, but overall it was not a bad result.

We were soon back in camp and we sent the wounded Gurkha off to the sickbay. He would in time, undoubtedly, be sent back to a hospital in Germany to recuperate and when he was recovered he'd be sent back to Nepal. At least he wasn't going home in a box, which made him one of the lucky ones. Many *did* get sent back home to Nepal in boxes. Not nice.

But watching those airstrikes had been amazing and demonstrated to me what truly awesome firepower the Americans had. There's no way I'd like to be on the receiving end of any of that! It had gone on for a good thirty minutes and it was truly compulsive viewing.

Chapter 5
CIA Safe House

My alarm went off at 06.00 and I didn't even hear it. I was totally knackered. We'd been on patrol until the early hours escorting a convoy of petroleum trucks down from Turkey again. I was awoken by Stu banging like fuck on my door and shouting about getting my lazy arse out of bed or I'd be late for breakfast. Now, to tell you the truth, my ideal morning routine, if I'm not going for a run or doing some gym work, is a nice, long, red-hot shower followed by two or three cups of coffee and some beans on toast. I had none of that this morning. I was late. I chucked on my trousers and T-shirt and legged it out of my room. It was still dark. I couldn't figure it out. Why was it still dark? Then it dawned on me: the other guys had sneaked into my room and altered my alarm clock by an hour and a half while we had been out on patrol. Then, when the other patrol had come in from another mission, they banged on my door at around 05.00. 'That'll teach you to take so fucking long in the showers Mercer!' Stu said, cracking up. 'Arseholes!' I said, slamming my door and getting undressed again. And then I thought, Fuck it! I might as well get into my patrol gear – normally a T-shirt, plain khaki combat trousers, desert boots and belt with pistol holster on it. I would come back for my hardware later (all my heavy stuff). At least I definitely had time for breakfast now, since there was absolutely no point in going back to bed. But I'd get my revenge.

Everything we carried on us, including weapons and ammo (which took up a hell of a lot of room), was kept in our rooms. With the hours we kept, an armoury would have been a pain in the arse. Obviously, we had one, but it kept to strict opening hours. Also, if the camp came under attack, I don't think there would be any way you could separate us from our guns. We had to be kept armed all of the time.

After my rude awakening, I took a brisk walk down to the mess hall past some huge conifer trees, planted for Saddam when he used to visit, and then past the constantly bustling helipad. I could make out an Apache gunship and a Black Hawk getting ready for takeoff; they looked like they meant business. The sun was coming up now and it looked to be another glorious day (apart from the bombing and shooting). I hadn't really heard any shooting yet – a rare situation – and it was almost peaceful. I hung around the helipad for a while because passing helicopters always fascinated me – probably something going back to my school-boy days. I could smell breakfast cooking and I was now feeling famished, so I made my way to the mess hall. You could always eat as much as you wanted – so we always used to train like hell.

I entered the mess hall and I could see there were troops covered in dirt and dust and looking knackered – they were obviously just in off some patrol. Then, in contrast, there were some troops looking clean but slightly apprehensive, probably because they were about to go out on patrol. And last, but not least, there were the desk jockeys, who always looked immaculate, as they were never required to leave the camp or even go out of the gate. After a great breakfast of poached eggs and beans on toast, I walked back to my room.

As I was walking along the main road six of our Toyota pickups approached, driven by our Fijian and Gurkha drivers. Every morning and night these guys would check the water and fuel and mount the heavy weapons on the trucks before our mission. It was quite a sight. They looked is if 'don't fuck with us' was written all over them. I jumped in one of the approaching vehicles through the open door and we drove down to our accommodation. I ran into my room and went through my routine: pistol in holster, body armour on, ammo pouches attached to body armour. OK, so the whole lot weighed a ton, but it was very comfortable when driving. I then put my rucksack on, which contained ten spare magazines of thirty rounds, so in total I was carrying around six-hundred rounds of ammunition. Then, lastly I picked up my M16 with M203 grenade launcher.

Wrapped around my M16 was a bandolier of twenty rounds of high-explosive 40mm grenades. I would always put these around my neck until I got to the vehicle. I turned my light out and kissed Kasper the dog bye-bye and, as usual, she tried to bite me. Little fucker!

I went to give my team a quick brief, do a comms check and make sure everything was ready. Once we were out of that gate there was no room for screw-ups. It all had to be slick as fuck. As usual, all the Fijian guys prayed, and I prayed with them. We could always do with all the luck we could get. We got the signal to mount up and assembled in a line of march – head of the patrol at the front, 2IC (second-in-command) in the middle. In the event that the lead vehicle was taken out, the 2IC would take charge. Every American soldier we saw on the way out of camp gave us a wave. We waved back. They knew that some of the time some of us wouldn't be coming back. Adrenalin was going some now as we approached the gate.

Each patrol commander pulled up his vehicle at the main entrance and we all got out. It always amazed me that not one of the guys was nervous. On the contrary, everyone was smiling and checking his kit. These were a fucking great bunch of guys, tough as you like, confident but not overly so. Last checks were made, then the command was given to load our weapons and make ready. I heard hundreds of loud clicks, almost in unison, ringing out (this was the guys cocking their weapons). We were ready to roll and got back in our vehicles and set off. The pace quickened and the wires and chains at the sentry post dropped. We flew past the concrete bollards and out we went out as we'd done so many times before. Not a round was fired at us, thank goodness!

We were to take a different route today and our main mission was to act as backup for another one of our call signs – they'd drawn the short straw and had a dangerous cargo of one hundred fuel tankers to protect. Our main job was to position our heavy weapons (the ones on the backs of our trucks) either side of the main dual carriageway on two opposite hills to protect their convoy, staggered so as to avoid a possible crossfire. We also positioned two vehicles as cut-offs, one up the road and one down.

As we tore through town, every one of us was checking his arc in anticipation of what could easily turn into a very bad situation. The main reason for this was that just outside town the CIA – or OGA (other government agencies), as they prefer to be known in Iraq – had a heavily fortified safe house on the outskirts of Mosul. This was guarded by some of our Gurkhas and the American security company Triple Canopy. This house was not that safe! It was constantly getting mortared and shot at by the insurgents, so driving past the bloody place always gave everyone the heebie-jeebies. There were some ideal ambush positions for the insurgents around this area, with high ground on either side of the buildings and the main complex. Unfortunately, it was the only road to and from our base, and insurgents could just as easily hit us at any time – as later on we would find out, big time.

We sped past the OGA building, which was now on our left, as fast as possible. We really did have to drive at breakneck speed. Everyone was tense, with thumb and fingers on their safety catch, at the ready. The heavy-weapon gunners on the back were equally ready, each gunner in each truck taking up arcs left and right. I was at the back this time, in control with the M19 automatic grenade launcher. This thing could bring down a house; it was a weapon definitely not to be used for warning shots! We also had two massive Fijians in the back seats with M240 GPMGs; we had some awesome firepower.

Once past the OGA (CIA) building we were then on to a dual carriageway with hills on one side and a 10-foot wall on the left. To all intents and purposes, we were travelling along a shooting gallery, and the insurgents knew this. However, this was the only way out of town and the insurgents also knew that, if they had a pop at us on this route, they would have twenty-four pissed-off Fijians or Gurkhas with bigger guns than they had, unleashing everything they had in return, so it was easier for them to fire at the Yanks. Now, the insurgents are far from stupid. They are extremely effective and intelligent. But they would often go for the easy target, and this we were certainly not. They knew they would have trouble on their hands if they went for us.

As we got past the worst part of the danger, my arse began to relax a bit and I took my thumb off my safety catch and switched on my sat-nav and switched off the bomb-jamming equipment. We'd done this journey many times before but, in the event of having to split the patrol, we had emergency RVs (rendezvous points) put into all the routes we took. All of this was put in code in case any insurgents managed to get hold of one of our vehicles. If a vehicle was disabled and we would have to leave it behind, we would blow it up to make it unusable.

We got deeper and deeper into the desert and there were now no signs of houses, just the occasional hut by the side of the road selling engine oil and truck bits. Soon we came up to our main positions. We then put the Toyotas into four-wheel drive and left the road – always a risk, as getting stuck in the sand can make you can easy target for a sniper. Three of our vehicles broke left and our three broke right. My group of three vehicles carried on for half a click (kilometre), then we got into our positions, facing towards the dirt tracks that insurgents could possibly have approached us by.

Now that we were in position, I posted a sentry with binoculars (whose job it was to scan the whole of the area we were covering to spot any potential trouble). We did a comms check again and surveyed the area. Nothing and no one (not even on foot) could approach us without our seeing them. We had ample cover from the road. In any case, we were supposed to be overt, not covert.

After we were settled and in position it was now around 08.30 and I was getting some funny looks from the Fijians. Fuck! They'd gone two and a half hours without eating and if they didn't eat soon I wouldn't be popular! 'Get stuck in, then,' I gestured. They didn't need to be asked twice. Those guys could really put away some food. After they had their feed they looked much happier. I felt better, too.

Because we were now pretty much in the desert and totally in the middle of nowhere, all the team leaders decided to let the lads have a bit of target practice with the heavy weapons. These are so powerful and formidable that there weren't any ranges around on the American camps that we could use to practise on, so when we had time, and it was safe to do so, we'd let our gunners let rip in the desert. Each team let each other's know what they were doing and we gave each other strict arcs of fire and identified some targets well away from each other. I chose an outcrop of rocks about 800 metres to our right. We were already made ready, so my gunner set his sights, took his safety off, then *boom, boom, boom*! Three rounds of 40mm high-explosive grenades went hurtling towards the rocky outcrop. He had almost a direct hit and a huge dust cloud rose up. A split second later we heard the impact (sound does take a while to travel). That was good enough for me. My gunner had one more burst and by then he'd obliterated the rocks. Target practice now over, we reloaded and then ate a few more snacks.

After about an hour and four cups of coffee, we heard over the sat phone that the other teams' mission had been cancelled, so they were now on their way back. Good news all around. This would mean we would maybe make a late lunch back on camp, which made the guys cheer up enormously. The other teams would be passing through our position in approximately thirty minutes, so we prepared to move. The plan was to let the other teams pass, then, fifteen minutes or so later, we would follow on. This would split us up and make sure that there wouldn't be twelve vehicles all travelling in a line – which would obviously make one mother of a target for an insurgent with his hand on a trigger to detonate an IED or for someone keen on ambush.

Twenty to twenty-five minutes later we could see the other teams approaching in the distance and, as they came past us, one of our lads mooned at them and the rest of us gave the finger – the usual sort of greeting that we gave to each other. We were always trying to have a laugh and a piss-take at every opportunity. It was a good way to destress. We briefly chatted to the other team on the radio and confirmed our plan. As they sped past we sat tight and watched them approach the outskirts of town. I was feeling hungry now and was looking forward to a nice lunch.

As we mounted up in our trucks we heard a loud boom in the distance, then saw a huge cloud of black smoke. My heart sank and I started to chant my mantra in my head, 'No! Fuck, fuck, fuck!' Then it came over the comms network. It was a broken message: 'Nine Zero Charlie, contact, wait out.' It was a contact report from our mates. They'd been hit. The other team were in deep shit: they'd been hit, and hit bad. That was one hell of an explosion they'd gone through and, if we could see it 5 kilometres away, it must have been a big bastard of a bomb – very bad. In a second we were off and trying to maintain radio silence. This was so that if the call sign in trouble needed to pass on information to the American HQ our comms chatter wouldn't interfere. Then came a message over the radio: 'Nine Zero Charlie, contact report: we've been hit by an IED outside the CIA building and are coming under effective enemy fire.' It is such a distressing, helpless feeling, to hear one of your call signs (your friends, your mates) in trouble and you're not there to help. There was thick black smoke billowing up into the sky now, and as we approached we could hear the firing, and lots of it! We had a lot of bother on our hands! We were going in to kick arse or get our arses kicked; we were heading into the unknown but we had to go – it was our friends in there!

We had to make a split-second decision: whether to go firm and wait for a request for assistance or go into the kill zone and assist. What a predicament! There could be nothing and nobody left alive to rescue in there. They could have all been taken out for all we knew. Fuck it! We were going in – it was our mates in there, right in the middle of that shit storm. We were all chomping at the bit and eager to go and help out when Frank, our patrol commander, gave the nod and that was it: safety catches off, and we were away. We could now see bits of the car that had obviously contained the IED. I could see the engine block, wheels, tyres and a big bloody crater where it had been. 'Watch and shoot lads!' I shouted. 'Any fucker with a gun who's not one of ours, kill 'em!'

We drove past the remains of the car and saw that there were a couple of clearly dead bodies (with limbs missing) nearby; it was pretty grisly. Then I saw a man on his knees, really distressed and with no shirt on, wearing only ripped trousers and covered in blood. When I looked closer I saw that his arm had been taken clean off. He was crying. He looked to be in a very bad way. He wasn't one of our guys. He may just have been an innocent passer-by – we didn't know and so we just went past him.

Then there was a blast of gunfire from my gunner in the back seat 'Enemy right, top of the hill, on the right!' he shouted. Then all hell broke loose. Our whole patrol was identifying targets and the amount of fire we were putting down was truly incredible. There was, fortunately, no sign of our other call sign in the area and I couldn't hear a damn thing on the comms because of all the gunfire. My gunner behind shouted, 'Enemy right,' again. We both turned around and I let off my M203 grenade launcher towards the wall, where an insurgent was clearly trying to escape over the top. I missed him by a mile but I blew a bloody great hole in the wall. (In my defence, I will say that that was the first time I'd fired an M203 in anger and we were on the move at the time.) My M240 gunner then let rip with a huge burst and I fired five or six rounds from my M16. The insurgent fucked over the wall in a spray of blood – it was messy. I figured that, because we travelled at speed, it would have been a better bet to try to use my grenade launcher and take him and the wall out, but after my first crap shot I found that my gunner already had him in his sights and sent him off to paradise (hope he got his virgins).

We sped through the kill zone as quickly as possible once we were sure our other call sign was definitely out of there and not in trouble. Then, as we rounded the corner, going up to the main road that led to the camp, we saw two Strykers (American armoured personnel carriers) coming towards us down the hill. We screamed to a halt and cordoned off the road. We took cover and scanned the area and then communicated with the Stryker commander what had happened. They seemed hesitant to help at first, but then they called in air support for us. There was still the odd round winging about (probably snipers) and I took cover by lying in the gutter behind a large kerbstone. There wasn't much to take cover behind and it was the best I could do. After air support was secured, I told my lads to keep popping the occasional round off into likely enemy positions, but to aim only at the high ground, no built-up areas, and to keep their heads down and not to take any stupid risks.

When we felt that the situation was under control, we jumped back into the trucks and continued our journey back to camp. Everyone was on a knife edge all the way back. We came through camp; there was no waving this time, just the American sentries scurrying about. They knew our predicament and were concerned for us. They knew we'd been in a big contact and had sustained casualties. Fair play to them.

We quickly unloaded all our weapons and checked that everything and everyone was OK. Apart from a few holes in the vehicles, we were fine, nothing drastic. We then drove to the ops room. As we pulled up outside we didn't know what to expect. We had heard no news, as there was a lot of confusion, so we didn't know what injuries or deaths had occurred with the other patrol. All the medics were legging it about outside the hospital and, from what we could see, one of the vehicles had been dragged in on its rims by an American Humvee. Its alloy wheels were ground down and its tyres were long gone, and there were bullet holes down one side. Everyone in that truck, miraculously, was fine, though. It was a very different story for 9.0 Charlie's command vehicle and crew.

I was still trembling with adrenalin as I got out of my vehicle. There was no smiling or laughing now – everyone was deadly serious and concerned.

I could see some bullet holes in the Land Cruiser that had been the command vehicle and there was a hell of a lot of blood everywhere, but no apparent bomb damage. I prayed that the occupants hadn't been too seriously hurt and I looked in the back seats (you have to remember there were no doors on our vehicles). It was obvious from the mess inside that one of the Gurkhas (or both) had been badly hurt or, worse, killed. There were obvious bone fragments in the footwells and on the back seat. There were bullet holes on both sides and a rip in the front passenger seat. But, as it turned out, one round had totally penetrated our armour and had passed through the back door, going right through the unfortunate Gurkha, and then carried on into the vehicle commander, Frank. As I was looking at the damaged vehicle I felt a tap on my shoulder. It was my boss. He told me that Frank had been shot in the right-hand side but he didn't know how bad it was. It was all very confused. You have to remember that we weren't bodyguard teams with armoured SUVs. We were carrying out a military role but more often than not without the military backup. It seemed crazy to some people.

From the limited information we had it looked like a few rounds (not many but enough) had hit the Toyota: one round hitting the Gurkha on the driver's side, the other going in through the back door then through the back seat and through the pelvis of the Gurkha, then carrying on through the back of the front passenger seat, hitting Frank in the right-hand side of his abdomen. I had looked at the bone and blood in the back seat and just assumed the worst, as it didn't look at all good.

The medics in the camp hospital (which was conveniently situated opposite our offices) were working hard to stabilise the two Gurkhas. Then we heard the great news that Frank was OK. He came out of the hospital holding his side, looking a bit sore and sorry for himself. 'Let's have a look then, you poof!' someone said. Frank lifted up his T-shirt to reveal a massive round bruise, which looked sore as hell. It looked to me as if he'd been hit with a squash ball! All the Fijians then gathered round and held hands and prayed, as they always did; everyone joined in. Even after the prayers, you could tell the lads were still worried about the two Gurkhas, though. There had, after all, been a lot of blood and bone.

We were then told to stand down and de-service all the kit. We'd got off 3,500 rounds of various types of ammunition on this contact, which is an incredible amount. This de-service included the vehicles, which would have to be checked over, and we also had to hose out all the blood. We didn't have any spare vehicles on camp so it was important that they were kept running and in as good order as possible. If one was really trashed or we'd had to blow one up, we'd just have to travel up to Turkey to buy another one.

After all the commotion, the prayers and the chin-wagging, all the team leaders then got together and we had a discussion to see if, with hindsight, we might have done things any differently. It was eventually concluded that the situation couldn't have been avoided; it happened, and nobody could have predicted or prevented what had occurred – it was just one of those things in this fucked-up place. We just had to move on.

After the trucks had been checked over, we drove down to our accommodation, all of us now in a bit of a sombre mood. I greeted Kasper the dog, unlocked my front door and went inside. I took off all my gear and then sat down on my bed and tried to mentally absorb what had just happened. I was still deaf as a post from all the firing. I couldn't hear a fucking thing over the ringing in my ears.

Also, I was still shaking from all the adrenalin – well not so much shaking as a gentle, tiny tremble. I still felt edgy and ready to go, though – my adrenalin was still pumping. I made myself a coffee and stripped my weapons down to clean them. I didn't feel hungry any more and we had a big debrief scheduled for 16.30, so I just put some chill-out music on and got on with my admin work.

If you don't keep M16s clean you can get quite a few stoppages, but they have a device fitted to them called a forward assist, which means that, if the round isn't located in the chamber correctly, you can hit this device with the palm of your hand and physically force the round into the chamber. This comes in handy. As with the British SA80, if you do get a stoppage, you have to go through the rigmarole of a stoppage drill. So I set about cleaning my guns. These were our life-lines.

Later that afternoon we had a call from one of the surgeons to say that both the Gurkhas would pull through. Apparently, one of them had a bad leg injury and the other had a shattered pelvis. Not good, but both guys would fly back to Nepal after being flown to a hospital in Germany. I felt much better after hearing that news. It picked my spirits up and I knew that everyone felt the same. Apparently, during the firefight, even after the terrible injuries they received, the two Gurkhas had refused to lie down and take it easy – no, not at all. They had carried on. Hard little fuckers, from witness accounts – they'd fought all the way back to the camp! They'd both lost a hell of a lot of blood and both had horrific injuries and they must both have been in terrible pain, but they had carried on fighting – incredible.

At 16.00 the same day, all the team leaders involved in the contact went up to the American citadel. We weren't allowed in there normally, because, being Brits, South Africans, Zimbabweans and so on, and therefore not US citizens, we couldn't be vetted by the US government for security clearance. Only the Yanks who were part of our outfit could get clearance. This was why our main boss was an ex-major in the US Special Forces, so he ran the show and he usually went to all our briefs. However, on this occasion, we had been given express permission from the top to get clearance for entry into this place. Something big was going on and I was about to find out what.

We all entered the citadel, which was situated inside one of Saddam's buildings and looked – and was – very grand. As we all looked around the place, an American soldier came up and spoke to our boss and all of us then followed him upstairs. At the top of a winding staircase we entered what must have been some sort of conference room. Everyone sat down and a big projection screen dropped down. What we were about to watch would blow our minds.

People were pouring in and the room rapidly became packed. There were probably around fifty people of all ranks, and we knew that whatever was about to happen was, obviously, of great importance, because we four team leaders were sitting in prime positions right at the very front, while captains and majors in the US Army stood at the back. But I suppose, after all, it was we who stood to get the crap blown out of us.

After everyone was settled the room fell silent and in walked four plain-clothes American guys. I recognised two of them as CIA and I assumed the other two were the same or from some other sort of government intelligence agency. They introduced themselves as OGA and started to explain the mystery of why we were all here.

First, before they went into their spiel about this mystery, they proceeded to show us a film. It was of our convoy coming under attack! It was obvious that it had been taken from CCTV footage from a camera outside the CIA safe house. At first, we couldn't believe what we were seeing. First of all, it showed the first and second Toyotas of the other call sign passing by their building, then, just as the third vehicle was going past, there was a huge fireball, and smoke covered the screen. We then saw the other vehicles taking evasive action. You could see the muzzle flashes from the weapons (there was no sound on the film), then they all took off. I then saw our patrol come bombing through. We all sat there in the room totally gobsmacked. The reason we'd been brought together, we were told, was that the OGA wanted to inform us that they'd known there was a bomb there and that we'd personally been driving past it every day for over three days! Wankers!

Then they showed us another film which they had shot over the previous three days. It made for incredible viewing. It showed three men pushing an apparently broken-down car towards the gates of this so-called safe house. Then they had left it parked right outside the entrance – and I mean right outside, next to the left-hand post of the gate. One man had then got down on his knees and stuck his hand under the rear bumper and then stood up again – he was obviously arming the bomb! The film was then fast-forwarded to the following evening and then the same three men appeared and again one got down under the bumper and, obviously, disarmed the bomb, unbelievable! Then they pushed the car out of the way. This routine went on for three days.

Unbelievably, the US military and CIA had known but hadn't informed us. The bomb had been meant for the CIA or US Army – so they'd just done their best to avoid it. We couldn't believe what we were hearing and seeing. We had been driving past that bomb for two days in a row. In the end the insurgents must have thought, What the hell! – and figured that they had been sussed, as the Yanks were clearly avoiding it, and had decided to have a go at us instead.

This was a massive, massive blunder and the lack of communication was infuriating. We were all fuming. We'd nearly lost three mates because of their incompetence or lack of care. We couldn't comprehend that they'd been watching this bomb being pushed in and out for days and the intel hadn't filtered down to us. Everyone, and I mean everyone, had known about this except us. Cheers, guys! There were lots of apologies that day and we set the wheels in motion to make sure something like that would never happen again.

We didn't have a body count for that day, either insurgent or civilian. It was confirmed that the guy I had seen on his knees with his shirt and arm missing had died. In hindsight, I should have finished him off – he was in a right mess – but I couldn't. I'm not put together like that. I couldn't kill an innocent unarmed civilian. Besides, we weren't paid to look after civilians, much as we'd sometimes have liked to. It was a really bad situation out there, but it was out of our hands, out of our control.

We did have one bit of luck that day. It seems that the American military were going to come in guns blazing until they knew and confirmed it was us. We could have been wiped out by both sides. So not a bad day for us after all, though I've got to say that we didn't feel particularly lucky, given the circumstances.

I'd had enough excitement for one day, so, after the usual debrief, we had a few beers and tried to relax. I then went to my room to watch some crap copied DVDs, and soon I was fast asleep.

The CIA safe house was getting a lot of attention from the insurgents now and, as I said, getting shot at daily and often bombed or mortared on a regular basis. The CIA were getting sick and tired of this and I'm sure the Gurkhas and Triple Canopy weren't too chuffed with the situation, either. Eventually, it was decided that the safe house wasn't safe any more, as it was becoming too dodgy. So we were tasked to go up there and stand guard while they blew all their stores up. It was unbelievable; they had decided that they were just going to put all their computers and delicate information in the house's cellar and surround it all with a load of plastic explosives and then detonate it – which would, it was hoped, just blow the crap out of everything in the place (and likely demolish most of the building as well).

Our job was to escort a civilian coach to the safe house and back again. After the normal mad dash across town, we tore through the gates and screamed to a halt in the compound. We discovered, when we arrived, that they already had all the wheels in motion. Everyone was already all packed up, the explosives were being laid and they were all ready to go – even all the Gurkhas, who would now be coming to work with us. Once the explosives were detonated the huge complex was just going to be abandoned. Anyone would be able just to go in and take it over – it wouldn't be long before squatters moved into any usable parts of the building that were left (there were a lot of homeless Iraqis).

We cleared the area and the spooks set about destroying their gear, which seemed like a waste to me but the information and equipment were, apparently, too sensitive to be moved. It was decided, higher up the chain of command, that if we'd crashed with it or lost any of it on the way back to camp, and it then fell into the insurgents hands, it would have been disastrous. Hence the decision to blow the crap out of the lot of it. I still thought it was an unnecessary waste, but you don't argue with the CIA.

The charges and explosives were set and everyone was ready for the off. These explosives were very hi-tech and we asked if we were needed to hang around and do the detonation, but we were informed that it was all going to be detonated by remote control once we were clear of the complex. Everyone loaded up and we tore out of the gates expecting the worst at any minute. It was a very tense moment, as the insurgents had lookout posts observing the complex and would obviously know that something big or at least out of the ordinary was going on. There was a very real chance of ambush.

All the Gurkhas and Triple Canopy guys were in their vehicles and we fled. All of a sudden there was a burst of gunfire, then another – we'd been sussed! As usual, it was hard to identify where the fire was coming from and we frantically scanned the area trying to pinpoint where the bastards who were trying to kill us were concealed. It was very dodgy to say the least. Then we heard the thunderous blast behind us – the CIA had obviously done the deed and blown the house.

Two rounds then hit our vehicle. Luckily, they struck our homemade armour on the driver's door and didn't penetrate it. It was definitely a case of so far, so good. We ploughed on with crossed fingers that we would not encounter any IEDs or mortars. So here we were, six of our vehicles, a busload of Gurkhas, one very scared coach driver, two trucks full of Triple Canopy guys and one vanload of CIA guys, and we were getting incoming fire. We were making a huge target of ourselves, which was not an ideal position to be in, but we'd been in worse before and at least we'd not been hit by an IED – not yet!

As we rounded a bend on our way back towards camp, we saw four insurgents legging it. That was it for our guys. They clicked straight into attack mode. As the insurgents were running, a hail of various kinds of bullets from our teams hit them in the back – it seemed as if everyone had opened up on them, all using different weapons. I can't even recall how many shots were fired but I know it was a lot, and it was over in moments. All four of these insurgents were killed, shot in the back. This is not strictly honourable but they had been shooting at us and all four of them were carrying weapons and seemingly hell-bent on killing us. They had AK-47s and RPK light machine guns, so they obviously weren't out for an afternoon stroll! I guessed that we'd surprised them in the act of setting up an ambush for us. Lucky for us; unlucky for them.

We were now much nearer the safety of camp and were just starting the approach when we had more incoming fire. Then my gunner on the back fired his M19. Now, when this thing went off, it made the whole truck rock and the explosions it caused were incredible. I bet those fucking insurgents didn't know what had hit them. The M19 was tearing chunks out of the hills they were hiding in. The insurgents had the element of surprise on their side – but that was it. With our superior firepower we soon had the upper hand. After my gunner had let rip with the automatic

40mm grenade launcher there wasn't much left of that cliff and – lo and behold! – all the incoming fire had stopped.

We carried on driving at breakneck speed, trying to make it back to camp in one piece. So far, so good – we'd had no casualties, not even any minor injuries. As we came haring back towards the gate, the sentries did the usual: they dropped the wires and chains and gave us a friendly wave; these sentries were all now our good mates.

As we pulled up, the unthinkable happened. We had all got out of the vehicles to unload, and the gunner on the back of my truck (the guy operating the M19 grenade launcher) also went to unload but he had forgotten that he still had one up the spout! Basically, he was still 'made ready', so when he fired off the action he fired the weapon, and it discharged a round. Well, it's policy and training to point your weapon in a safe direction when you're unloading it, in the event that, if you fuck up your drills and forget (which he had) and do an accidental discharge, you won't shoot and kill someone.

My gunner, probably down to all the adrenalin from the recent contact, didn't carry out his drills correctly. He went to clear the weapon and fired off a round of high explosive into fuck knows where! These things have a range of approximately 1,500 metres, so it could have gone anywhere. Some poor fucker, or family, could have had a rude awakening – or even worse.

Not one of the Brits I worked with out there had ever had an ND (negligent discharge), but, then again, we were supposed to be far better trained than most. It is far better to have an ND into a sandpit at the gate than to launch some sort of high-explosive projectile into the unknown. This was a monumental fuck-up. However, because we weren't military, he couldn't be charged. As punishment for his mistake, what we did was give him all our really shit chores to do for the next week. We had to be seen to do something.

That incident reminded me of when I was working with the Royal Ulster Constabulary (now called the Police Service of Northern Ireland) in Belfast when I was a young marine. We (our team of marines) had a cottage just across the road from the camp pub. It was a pub mainly for the forces on camp. That evening we'd just come off patrol and had headed straight for the pub while the RUC officers had gone into our cottage to make themselves a few cups of tea (this wasn't out of the ordinary, as we let them use the kitchen), when one of the RUC officers went to unload his weapon. He did this in the kitchen and had pointed his Browning 9mm pistol towards the ceiling, then fired off the action, but he still had one up the spout. The result, because of his fuck-up, was that the round that he discharged went up through the ceiling and straight through both legs of one of my mates. Incredibly, our mate was so pissed that he was still asleep and totally unaware that he had been shot.

The RUC officer came running over to the pub, where we were drinking in the bar, and told us what had happened. We were all a bit drunk and we thought, to begin with, that he was just trying to wind us up. He eventually managed to convince us that he was serious and we all ran back over the road to the cottage. We charged up the stairs and into the bedroom and found Simon still drunk, very much fast asleep and totally unaware that he had been shot.

That particular RUC officer was subsequently removed from the firearms squad while an inquiry was launched. Don't know what happened to him after that, but it goes to show the damage that can be done when the proper procedures are not strictly adhered to.

Anyway, back to Iraq. With everyone safely through the gate now we could chill and hopefully get some nice food. The Yanks had just had a food resupply, so we knew that the grub was going to be good for a while at least. On our way to the chow tent we dropped off the guys and all our major weapons back at our accommodation.

Then, just to really piss us off, we heard the sound of incoming mortars. Those fucking insurgents never let up. They were always having a pop at us in some way or another. We all legged it for cover. I heard three more rounds strike but by that time we were safely inside our air-raid shelter, which also doubled as the Gurkhas' kitchen. We heard another three rounds drop. We were just going to hang tight, safe in our shelter, but then we heard that some of the American soldiers on camp had been injured.

Because of our close ties, and friendships, with the American military our medics decided to go and offer whatever help they could. They ran up to the hospital to help out. We waited in the shelter until the mortars stropped coming down.

Later, the medics came back to tell us that nobody had been killed in the strikes but that there had been some very nasty injuries. Mortar strikes on camp were quite common but were, more often than not, ineffective. It was rare to get injured on camp. Those American soldiers had just been very unlucky.

Chapter 6

Shopping in Kurdistan

Shopping trips in Iraq are non-existent. Only crazy nutters have tried it. However, in Kurdistan (as I'll call it for the purposes of this book) it's possible. Kurdistan is an area situated right up in the northernmost part of Iraq, very close to the Turkish border. Shopping is possible here for many reasons, one of which is that it's ruled with a fist of iron by the Kurds and, if you're an Arab or an insurgent, you'll be found out (they have their own clandestine ways of finding this out – some legal, some not so).

The Kurds are a different breed and they run their part of Iraq totally differently from the south. They run the place with efficiency and with very little violence. They have their official and unofficial ways of policing this, but it seems to work for them. I'm not saying there's no violence, but compared with the rest of Iraq they seemed pretty well sorted. Whenever we entered Kurdistan, we were always welcomed with a wave and a smile by everyone. The local kids used to run up to us full of curiosity and questions. What I found amazing about the kids we came across up there was that they all seemed to speak English perfectly.

We often went up through there on our way up into Turkey to buy vehicles, to replace ones that we'd had to blow up or had been shot to bits. We'd travel peacefully through the Kurds' territory and then on to the Turkish border. Once you got just past the border there was, unbelievably, a Toyota dealer – he was our main man. We'd turn up, as always, armed to the teeth, but we were inside Turkey and so we were pretty safe. We'd hand over £25,000 or $55,000 in cash. Then we had to drive the Hilux, Land Cruiser, whatever, back through Kurdistan and then back through Mosul; but the unlucky driver of the new vehicle had no armour and no guns on the back. All he had were a couple of crazy Fijians sitting in the back with M16s, but we still had the doors on, which wasn't good – not for them at least.

Once, we'd managed to get the truck back to the camp, the doors were soon taken off and the welding torches and cutting tools came out and it was A-Team time. It looked so very funny: just as in the old *A-Team* TV series, we even had our own Bosco ('BA') Baracus, in the shape of this giant Fijian (though he didn't wear quite so much bling as BA) and it goes without saying that we had plenty of crazy fools!

Huge plates of steel were then welded onto the back to protect the gunner, and more plates were welded inside the driver's door. It was fucking mental. Our vehicle area on camp looked like a scrapyard: there were smashed windows in every corner plus hundreds of wheels, dozens of doors and quite a few trashed vehicles. We had no qualified vehicle mechanics on our team, just guys who had learned a few skills in their home countries by doing a bit of DIY. But I tell you what: it all worked. Considering the number of contacts we went through, we were effective. Our homemade armour worked, and it worked very well. Considering we had to be self-sufficient and were working in this fucking dangerous place with little or no Yank support, I think we were doing OK.

Up in Kurdistan we could relax though. We'd park up and go through the market stalls, just wearing our body armour and pistols. It was hilarious when you could go into a supermarket, which were all equipped with metal detectors on the doors, and we obviously had our pistols and spare magazines on (some of the lads still carried their M16s), but the staff would just give us a smile and a wave and let us through, which always sent the metal detectors beeping like mad. There was nice subdued music and local people out doing their daily or weekly shopping pushing trolleys around. Then we'd walk in wearing body armour, helmets and weapons! It must have been truly an absurd sight to behold, but I suppose that, because these people had been brought up with war and had had a tyrant for a leader for many years, they were used to the sight of guns and armed personnel. It seemed to me that not a lot fazed these people.

We spent as much time as possible in Kurdistan because

of the tranquillity we enjoyed and the friendliness shown by the local people towards us. Kurdistan became our own safe haven, a place to have a calm moment and a relaxing time. There was a local restaurant that we would often frequent, which always served us great food – in fact as much as we could eat for about $20. Shopping was a bit like being on holiday in Turkey, with people hassling you to buy stuff (which could be a bit of a nightmare with the more persistent market stallholders).

There were always kids crowded around us trying to look at and touch our guns. They seemed very intelligent and were usually very smartly dressed. These kids were always pleasant and polite – more than can be said for some of the kids back home in the UK. As we often travelled up to that part of Kurdistan, some of the kids became familiar to us and we became quite attached to some of them and built up something of a rapport. It was certainly relaxing and refreshing to come to this part of Iraq and chill, because we all knew with certainty that when we left we were going back to a very bad place and we didn't know if all of us were going to make it. We seemed to run this gauntlet almost daily. Not nice but essential.

But walking and browsing through the Kurdistan markets was truly amazing. The hustle and bustle, the people, the stalls – you could have been in a place anywhere in Europe. The people up there were relaxed and living in harmony – a harmony they had created themselves. So here we were having a bit of relaxation and chilling out from the carnage of work in northern Iraq, knowing that the journey back would be no picnic.

On the market stalls you could buy anything, and I mean anything. It seems that a lot of the supply trucks for the US military would be attacked by the insurgents and the booty from these raids would end up on some of these market stalls. I knew that all of this was not necessarily legal or just, but I was just doing my bit to support the local economy and I was a mercenary, so what the fuck! At the end of the day, whatever was nicked, stolen, call it what you will, it was going to end up in some market, somewhere, somehow, so we'd be fools not to buy it, and if we didn't buy it someone else would. Trucks were getting raided and blown up all the time, so it really didn't make any difference.

In war-torn Iraq, you could buy anything – AK-47s for $50, Uzis for $100. However, it was mainly in Kurdistan that we'd stock up on satellite phone equipment and beer. And we would always try to incorporate a trip here if our missions took us anywhere near the area. As soon as we were given a mission to go near to Kurdistan and we arrived in one piece, it was happy days.

On one occasion, as we started our travels back from Kurdistan, I witnessed one of the weirdest things I have ever seen in a danger zone in my life. There were two cyclists in the middle of the desert, fully kitted out with state-of-the-art bicycles, looking for all the world as if they were taking part in the Tour de France – it was wicked! These two guys were tanking along and as we overtook them I shouted a warning.

'Do you guys know you're heading into fucking Mosul?'

'Yeah – we live there,' was the reply!

These lads must have been very powerful (probably religious clerics of some sort) but they were fit and were firing along at a rate of knots all the same. Still it was so unbelievable to see these two immaculate cyclists wearing all the top gear going along a desert road towards the most dangerous place on the planet! Truly outstanding.

Along our route back to Mosul we passed a huge dam. It was built to provide hydroelectricity and apparently supplied most of northern Iraq's power. It really was most impressive and beautiful to look at. There is, surprisingly, a hell of a lot of water in Iraq, most of it found in the natural lakes, but they built big dams to store even more.

On one return trip we were travelling back into the very bad bandit country that could possibly and probably would seal some of our fates – nothing nice. Next thing, bollocks! Bang, bang, boom! Our truck in front swerved – another contact, maybe, or it could just be a puncture, but maybe not. This time it was only a small roadside device that had almost missed us, but we survived again with no apparent casualties – a few cuts and bruises but nothing terminal. It had been a very small IED. Yet again, we had been travelling too fast to notice it. It seemed amazing but we could find nothing to retaliate against. We ended up having to stop, as it turned out the lead vehicle was actually shagged. While the IED hadn't damaged any of the guys inside, it had, unfortunately, knackered the vehicle. We went into all-

Above: This is the ordnance we found in the back of a taxi which attacked our base. None of the insurgents survived.

Below: An Apache attack helicopter escorting us. It's nice to have that kind of backup!

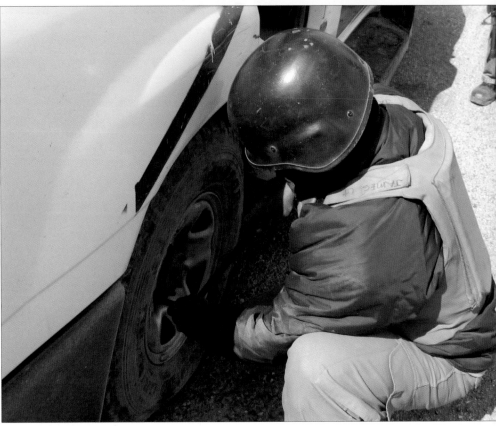

This is where the mad Gurkha changed the wheel in the middle of a firefight in Tal Afar. Incredible.

Above: Having a casual day – and boy did we need it.

Below: Practising contact drills.

Above: Weapons training.

Below: When you let loose with the Mk19 grenade launcher all hell breaks loose. You can take out entire buildings.

Above: Practice makes perfect, and with an automatic grenade launcher you need to be lead on.

Below: The problem with off-road is that sometimes you end up in the shit.

Above: More contact drills in the desert – we honed them so we could be as effective as possible.

Below: Me and the team in front of a US Army Black Hawk helicopter.

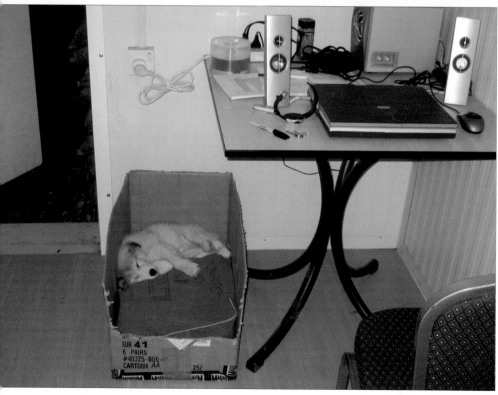

Above: Doing a beer run for the lads in Kurdistan.

Below: Our feral dog, Kasper. I adored the little sod but she always tried to bite me.

Above: A typical IED – I managed to grab my camera after I heard the explosion.

Below: We'd been hit by an IED, then ambushed. Two of our guys were killed. A very bad day.

around defence mode yet again while we put some plastic explosive in the vehicle and trashed it, then got the hell out of the way. However, we didn't get permission to do this, so we'd probably be in for another bollocking from the boss. We were going through pick-up trucks as if there were no tomorrow (up to that point in 15 months the job up north had gone through 27 vehicles).

You do get used to situations like this. It's funny, but when I arrived in northern Iraq I didn't think I could ever get used to it and now that I'd been up here for only a few months (but what seemed like ages) the case was far from it. I was now having a sick and twisted form of fun – call it a downward spiral, call it whatever you like, but I was having an adventure, and a prosperous one at that. I was enjoying most of this.

Once the vehicle was blown to bits we were slightly in the shit because, as I said before, we were supposed to get permission before doing this kind of shit. You can't just go blowing up £25,000–40,000 vehicles with no authority or permission. On this occasion we just didn't have the time to call back to base, or I think maybe it was because we'd lost our comms; I'm not sure what the problem really was. We just left the truck on the side of the road – fucked, no use to anyone, blown to bits. We had to shuffle everyone about to fit in the guys from the now useless vehicle, which made us a bit cramped, but we just wanted to get back to the relative safety of our enclosure on camp and have some nice food (depending upon the chefs), maybe a beer or two then watch a crap copied DVD or something similar. Life was never boring at least – always an adventure.

Chapter 7
Route Recce

One morning we were summoned to see our boss. It was obviously something quite serious. When we turned up at the ops room we were told we'd been given a new task to perform: Route Recce. We all looked at each other and thought, What the hell do they mean by that? Route Recce for whom, what and where? Turns out we were going out looking for insurgents! We had been given the power by the military to go out and do VCPs (vehicle checkpoints), which meant, basically, that we had taken on a small military role. We all knew the difficult role we'd been given by the Yanks but it was something new, maybe a bit different. Suicide bombers love VCPs: easy to creep up on unchallenged, then they can just let rip with their bombs. We could all become sitting ducks yet again.

Our new task would take us through places of interest clearing the routes or making it known to the insurgents that we or the US military had a strong presence in the area – searching them out almost.

A lot of these insurgents weren't even Iraqis: they were Egyptians and Syrians who had been paid to attack and fight the Coalition forces.

At that time, the insurgents had taken over nearly all of the police stations in Mosul and northern Iraq. Our instructions from the top of the military chain of command were not to stop for any checkpoints and to kill any person wearing a police uniform who tried to stop us. At this delicate time, eight times out of ten these would involve the bad guys. That put us in a very tricky position: we could very possibly waste the bad guys every time, but we would risk doing in a good Iraqi copper who was just trying to do his job (a very difficult one at that) in rebuilding his screwed-up country. This was a catch-22 situation. We had ourselves a predicament.

There are a lot of good people in Iraq and most of them want change. They had welcomed the Coalition forces but the situation for them hadn't improved with the removal of Saddam Hussein. In fact, for a lot of ordinary people regularly caught up in the crossfire and seeing their homes destroyed, it was probably worse. Some are just waiting numbly in their huts for the next dictator or tyrant to come along; and, because of the poverty and terror that they've been through, half the people just want to get on with life and don't seem to give a toss who runs the country. They just want a secure life. All they need is to be able to put food on the table for their loved ones. It seems to me that if you constantly hammer, torture and generally threaten a race of people over so many years they will succumb to anything. Things need and have to change sometimes, but it wasn't up to us to do it; it wasn't our job to bring change. Nevertheless, we were all concerned about the situation; you wouldn't be human if you didn't care.

We needed a new form of strategy now as we were crossing the line from bodyguard to potential mercenary. We were going to become the Yanks' bitches, but we didn't care. It just meant more action and more money. We'd get £50 a day more – not a lot but money's money. It still worked out at nearly £2,000 a year extra.

Some of the companies I have worked for out in Iraq are so huge and powerful that they can change governments. I can't and won't talk about the companies I've operated for in Iraq, but I will say, and can say, that, for instance, Blackwater have almost twenty-thousand troops on call and twenty aircraft. Truly an amazing force to be reckoned with, which could overthrow certain powers.

The US forces' special-ops teams in Iraq used to operate very similarly to us, moving fast, using soft-skinned vehicles with no doors on, but they moved only at night. They had up-to-date Level 6 shit-hot night-vision goggles, infrared capability, heat-detection equipment and other stuff. All we had were just the mad, nutty and brave little Gurkhas and the huge Fijians, willing to do anything at any time. We were, after all, hired guns, just there to keep the official death toll down. After what had happened to the four Blackwater guys who were torn apart by an angry mob in Fallujah when they were ambushed in March 2004, we needed to be fucking careful doing what we were doing. Taking on these jobs, as every PMC in war zones does, can seal your fate, and I don't mean in a good way. At the end of the day your only aim is to come back in one piece and be able to spend your dosh back home and, if you've got one, to spend time with your family.

As I said, we were told the police were dodgy (we knew this from intelligence received from the CIA). The northern police commander's official response was that 30 per cent of his officers were corrupted to some extent – not necessarily with insurgents but definitely affected by their presence.

Up to this point we'd been in quite a few contact situations, and we were having guys injured and killed on jobs, so we started buying some of our own kit – just to try to improve it a bit, really. Not that the kit issued to us was inferior, but it was just that some of it could be improved upon. Most PMC companies in Iraq supply Level 3 chest and back plates in their body armour, which will stop most projectiles, but we were issued with Level 5, which meant our vests could stop 7.62mm high-velocity rounds. However, these vests could become uncomfortable over rough ground and, since we used to take to the rough ground and desert as often as we could (because using these tactics made life for the insurgents far more difficult –

harder to predict our movements and, therefore, harder to ambush us), the discomfort was ever present.

So, with our mates in the US Special Forces, a few of us swapped beer with them and acquired some of their body armour – it's the same quality as ours but it's a lot more comfortable to wear, and you can attach your magazine pouches to it, so doing away with the need for ammo webbing or vests. But, at the end of the day, it always comes down to personal preference.

Some guys, especially the ex-US Special Forces members of our company, bought their own telescopic sights with heads-up capability. Basically, with a normal sight you shut one eye – right or left, it doesn't matter. With these heads-up sights you look through them with both eyes open. You can still see your target and still aim correctly. A very clever, effective piece of state-of-the-art kit. Try buying one of these fucking items in the UK and you'll get a loud knock at the door from the plods, who think you must be a terrorist. The Americans are far more liberal and they can buy anything and still get it into Iraq.

We exploited this to the max. The Yanks used to get us anything from porno mags to personal sights and shotguns. I worked with one US Special Forces guy who even carried his grandfather's pistol from World War Two and he'd just taken it over there with him.

Now that our equipment was more up to speed and more suited for our new tasks, we were ready to go, and, so long as the Gurkhas had a few shots of whisky on an evening and the Fijians got fed, we were sorted. I'm not saying for one instant that the Gurkhas were drunks; rather it was their end-of-day-perk – they certainly earned it.

Checking Iraqi security forces positions was going to be one of our primary tasks. This was to ensure that they were (a) providing a decent and proficient presence and (b) they were actually there! It was, to most of them, just a means of earning some sort of an income, and an easy one at that. Most of them weren't very committed to the job and to make matters worse a lot of them weren't at all reliable, either. I think, personally, that Iraq will take a very long time to rebuild because a lot of the men in the country care only about themselves, no one else. Even though hostilities officially ended on 16 April 2003, I don't think the country will be able to pick itself up for at least another few decades and maybe never. You now have the US military, the British military and us lot (about fifty thousand PMCs) running around this poor country. Who wouldn't be confused and pissed off? It is certainly going to take one hell of a long time to sort out the mess that is now Iraq.

I've never in my life done a job as intense as this one. Baghdad was a breeze compared with this line of work we were doing up in the north. And I probably never would, with hindsight, go back to a job as mad as this. I would definitely go back to being a bodyguard but nothing like the job or missions we encountered up in the north. It was sometimes pure carnage there. PMCs can be used for most purposes and if the money's right I'll do most things. As in

John Geddes' book, he drove around Iraq on his own, the mad bastard. I really take my hat off to him. I've a lot of respect for that man. It sounds gung-ho but it's true. It all depends upon whom you're working for mostly, but if it was legal (or nearly) we'd consider it; and if it was viable we'd fucking do it! There are probably a lot of professionals reading this who would say different. But, as I said, if the money's right, why not?

However, this day could be a different kettle of fish. We were armed to the teeth, as usual, and we were now on this new mission. Out through the gate we went, firing along at breakneck speed, trying to keep everyone safe and not blown to bits. We approached the first checkpoint, always difficult, but the Yanks just let us through. After that, fuck it! It was definitely mainstream dangerous for us.

Our new missions were now changing. We were now hunting down the insurgents – not just keeping a lookout for them, but actively hunting the hunters. Anyone targeting us or Coalition forces was fair game. We could take them out, no questions asked. We were, in fact, now undertaking offensive missions. We were now mercenaries, but we were all comfortable with it.

Now that our company was 'unofficially, officially' attached to the US military as a unit, we were very much one of their major assets. We were officially disposable troops. We had no casualty records, no fatality records, in fact no records at all. We could kill and be killed and no one would ever know or care.

Because the firing-range time with the Yanks was limited and mainly because of the immense firepower we carried, we had to do our own range, test and adjust routine in the desert because it was a lot safer this way. So this time when we went out on patrol we decided to stop and do a bit of target practice. This was normally done by taking water bottles out to approximately 1,000 metres; then the new guys would fire their M16s at the bottles; then a few of the rest of us would also have a go, if we thought we needed a refresher. Then the chain of weaponry would go up: M249, M240s and so on – you get the picture. And we were probably the most professional outfit in northern Iraq at that time. We were definitely the most heavily armed. We were the only company authorised to have automatic grenade launchers and .50-cals at that time. Because of the nature of our job, the US Army General in charge of everything and everyone thought the world of us and eventually became a good friend to us and gave us a lot of support. He, in fact, gave us the power to carry anything we wanted.

As we now gathered a little momentum in our tasks and were trying this mad new job as mercenaries, it became clear that a lot of us were probably going to peg it at some stage because this was such a high-risk and dangerous mission. Our newfound job – one of them, anyway – was, as we've seen, to assist in VCPs. We would need to stop random vehicles or suspects, search them and arrest them if we found something illegal. This would normally be a role for the military. However, we were given this task and we'd do our best to be humane and compassionate but, of course, deadly effective.

One morning as we started patrolling along the main highways, we were, as usual, staggered along the route at a few hundred metres apart. One of our patrols then headed off up into the mountains to reconnoitre the route ahead of us, when the other patrol, which had been instructed to go up into the mountains to do some surveillance and had gone off road up there, suddenly found itself in a contact situation. The comms crackled, 'Contact, wait out.' Fuck this was always bad. We'd never encountered a mild contact in Iraq. You just didn't. Everything was normally bad or very bad and usually involved IEDs or ambush by gun-toting insurgents who were normally armed to the teeth and trying to take you out in a hail of bullets.

One of the Toyotas, in the other patrol ahead of us, had gone across a dirt track and crossed through a wadi and, unfortunately, in doing so had gone over and compressed a landmine; this in turn had blown one of the Gurkhas in the rear right section of the Toyota up into the roof, the explosion almost ripping the vehicle and our poor Gurkha colleague in half. He was, unfortunately, killed instantly. Our medic did all he could. He tried for almost thirty minutes to resuscitate him, but to no avail. The device had gone off underneath where he was sitting and had blown him upwards into the roof of the Hilux. The force had totally snapped his neck, but I was told by a medic that it was his internal injuries that had killed him. However, the three remaining Gurkhas in the

131

vehicle had, incredibly, survived, but were in a deep state of shock. Because our US military backup was limited, we often didn't have the means to find out what ordnance had taken us out, so most of the time we just had to get out of the area. This put us in a dilemma, as we didn't know what to expect, but on this occasion we had to rendezvous with the Gurkhas to collect them and get them all safely back to base. We were all well aware that we could be hit by backup ambush devices. We were in a bad situation.

We arrived at the site of the explosion. It didn't seem to be the usual sort of device we encountered, but it had still made a right old mess. However, one of the guys in the patrol was a hardened ex-SAS veteran of some twenty-two years' service and had served in quite a few conflicts (most of the modern-day ones, in fact) and he said he'd seen these devices, or similar, in the First Gulf War. It may well have been left over from then; on the other hand, it may not.

Anyway, we had another man dead on our hands. We rearranged ourselves to accommodate the three traumatised Gurkhas and loaded our poor dead colleague onto the back of one of the trucks alongside the gunner. We considered what to do about our truck – it seemed totalled (unusable). We briefly discussed towing it back to camp but decided it wasn't salvageable, and nor was it worth the risk of having it slow us down and make us even more vulnerable to attack, so we just blew the fuck out of it to prevent it falling into insurgent hands.

Our death toll was rapidly rising.

Although if we had to leave a vehicle it was our standard operating procedure to blow it to bits, this time it was done for us. The Hilux was well and truly fucked. The mine had ripped it in half.

It was a sombre group that eventually returned to camp. The American sentries on the gate could tell as we approached that something had gone wrong, as they could see we were a vehicle down, and the usual smiles and waves were absent, although they did shout concerned questions to us as we passed through the gates. Once we were on camp the first thing we did was to make arrangements for the Ghurkha's body to be taken care of. Once that was arranged, we went in search of beer – and lots of it! It had been one hell of a day and we all needed a drink to settle us.

We managed to get hold of a few crates of beer and we went down to the accommodation and de-rigged. We didn't even bother to shower. We just wanted to sit down and chat over a beer about our departed friend. We lit a big fire and then we toasted our colleague and tried to get as wasted as we could, but not so wasted that we wouldn't be able to function in the morning, as this job was non-stop.

This was a rather grim and unofficial tradition among us if we ever lost a mate, a bit like holding a wake, I suppose. It is never easy to lose a friend or colleague, especially one who, on numerous occasions, had saved your arse or whom you'd fought alongside. So we spent the night drinking to him, basically drowning our sorrows, and remembering every funny thing or humorous incident involving him that we could because we knew that the next day we would have to get up and carry on with our job. It seemed to help numb the pain of our loss, anyway. We all just hoped that the next evening our colleagues would not be toasting us, which was a very real possibility in this line of work. We all shed a few tears that night.

As I've said before, the Yanks on camp thought we were nuts, driving along with no doors on. And, if we were in Baghdad or Basra, we would be nuts, but, then, back in Baghdad or Basra we would have been in armoured SUVs. Up here in the north, however, we were in a different ball game. At any time you might have to alight from the trucks fast and get the hell out at a moment's notice; and, because our trucks were all soft-skinned, our options were limited. We had to be quick on our toes and so it had been decided that the doors would just slow down our exit from a vehicle in an emergency contact situation.

I have mates who operate for other companies and work in Baghdad in pairs, using an Iraqi driver and passenger as cover. The bodyguards lie down in the back seat with blacked-out rear windows, using mirrors to see out with. These guys aren't nutters, they are the top earners (up to £1,000 a day). But, if you think about the situation that they are in, it's not that crazy. Their losses were far smaller than ours and, unless they were to break down in the city, they would normally be OK. However, I don't want to take anything away from them or imply that their job is easy. It's not. It's still a very dangerous job. We always kept in touch via email or mobile phone and compared notes about our different jobs.

Part of the new mission that we'd been given was to escort a US military psy-ops unit out. This is a complex specialised unit designed to try to win over the local communities by attrition – hearts and minds – basically winning the war by guile and not by strength. It was a tactic first employed by the Americans during the Vietnam conflict.

This was the first time civilian contractors were carrying out operations involving US military personnel. We were now transporting these US special-ops people around one of the most dangerous places on the planet. I don't know if it was official or unofficial, but we were doing it anyway. On the bright side, we now had full US military air support and state-of-the-art tactical support, and we could access their comms, which made a huge difference to us.

I don't know if this was a good thing or a bad thing. By taking on this role it could become a double-edged sword. This was truly getting very serious, but our relationship with the military was exceptional and I prayed that this would expand and continue. We had now been placed in the position of being responsible for the welfare and safety of some of the ordinary American troops and even some of their special-ops teams. This was quite daunting: to think that the US military's safety and security were now firmly entrusted to our hands, a private military contracting company. We were now responsible for a big important chunk of the American assets.

When we were training the Americans used to look to us because we were all ex-Royal Marine Commandos, SAS, SBS, French Foreign Legion, British Army, ex-Paras and so on. They started observing our tactics, almost studying them. A few American patrols took on our tactics, hard-targeting, debussing when stuck in traffic, etc. Taking the Yank special-ops guys on patrol was funny: they had all the gear you could think of and we were driving them around in soft-skinned Toyotas with no doors on! I think most of them just did it for the buzz; I think they secretly enjoyed riding with us.

Because we did such a fantastic covert and overt job, and had no rules of engagement, we could basically shoot at anything that became a threat to us without having to do reports. The Yank special-ops guys loved coming out with us. They had no contact reports to file, nothing; they were living and loving every bit of the life of a mercenary, with all the soldiering but none of the bullshit paperwork. They couldn't get enough of it and we liked having them along with us because they, as I said, had their comms and could call in air support if we needed it.

On our first run-out, we had to travel south to an airstrip that was just south of Mosul and was about an hour's dash away on a good run (two hours on a bad one). We just had to drop some guys off. We came in through the gate and had to stop to get directions, as this place was so huge. The airport had loads and loads of aircraft hangars and we didn't have a clue where we were supposed to drop these guys off – and they didn't know either.

We had arrived at the airport via the back entrance of the most northern runway next to this huge complex of buildings. This place was probably about the size of Gatwick Airport – that's pretty big. What was very apparent to us as we approached the runway was that there was a C-130 Hercules sitting in a hole! Apparently, when the American plane landed, no one had shared with the poor pilots the news that there was a big fuck-off hole in the runway caused by bomb damage. The poor pilots literally just taxied into it! There was a parked Humvee in the back of the C-130, which survived totally unscathed, but that was it. Everything else in the plane was well and truly broken. After the accident the Yanks turned up with their bomb-disposal unit and equipment and just blew the plane to pieces – after the explosion there was nothing left, just bits. What a monumental fuck-up. Seems the norm in Iraq is just to blow the crap out of anything, sad but true. But I suppose it is better to be safe than sorry, and, anyway, the Yanks love their explosives.

On the way back from having witnessed the demise of what to me had looked like only a slightly dented Herc, we were going to check out an Iraqi security position. So when we turned up – it was absolutely hilarious – these guys were armed to the teeth, but not from being supplied by the Iraqi army. No, these were weapons that they had kept or stolen from the First Gulf War. One guy had his own RPG painted in different colours and said he was saving it for a special occasion. What that occasion was I don't know! These guys were nice and friendly and of Kurdish origin so we didn't have to worry too much about our safety with them.

As we came back we had to go through a police checkpoint. We'd been warned about them; they'd been warned about us; hopefully, there were going to be no worries. Safety catches off, trigger fingers ready. I just hoped we wouldn't slot an innocent civilian. We were, after all, working in no-go areas, areas that most private military security companies were not allowed to work in, so the chances were that there was going to be civilian collateral damage of some sort along the way if we had a firefight. None of us were warmongers or animals, far from it. We were men with compassion and values, but we were also men in Iraq getting paid to do a dirty job – and I'm not talking about cleaning the bog! We were all there by choice. Good or bad, we were there trying to earn a crust (albeit a big one).

As we charged through the first checkpoint there was no opposition, thank goodness – or so we thought. Then there was a sudden burst of gunfire and we were on our toes. As we've seen, the worst thing about the contacts you encounter in the north is that it's difficult to identify where the fire is coming from. Identifying the fire point is often the hardest part, but once you've got this sussed you can rake the fuck out of them. We then saw two guys in police uniforms doing a runner. If they *were* police, surely they wouldn't be running away, AK-47s in hand. We couldn't be certain, so we let them live. Later on this would not be the case.

As we were driving white Toyotas and because these trucks are so reliable, the insurgents used them, too – same colour, everything, but without the heavy weapons. This could put the American pilots in quite a predicament when it came to identifying enemy targets or friendlies, like us. As we closed in on the camp, though still a few kilometres away, the unthinkable happened: we got lit up by a Yank patrol. Basically, we were fired upon by the Americans! It wasn't bad but it was enough to scare the shit out of us.

We had a blown out front tyre, scary enough though when you've got the might of the American military machine bearing down on you. We limped back to camp and went straight to the citadel, something had to be done to prevent a blue-on-blue situation like this happening again. The Americans apparently thought we could have been insurgents and lit us up. We were carrying no ID. Because of the confusion involved in any firefight, these situations could be even more difficult: our guys could have fired back, which would have been catastrophic. We were all armed to the teeth, and so were the US military. Ultimately, they would have won and we would have been wiped out. This situation could not be allowed to happen again.

After an emergency meeting it was decided that at night, if we had to travel, we were going to be issued with infrared strobes: flashing lights visible from 20 miles but not to the naked eye. Only the Apache and Black Hawk pilots with night-vision goggles could see us. In the daytime we would employ the hi-tech method of putting massive, fuck-off fluorescent orange flags on the roofs or bonnets of the trucks!

I have a lot of respect for these pilots who risk their arses, but I am still paranoid about incoming friendly fire, and we faced this prospect daily, especially with new American military units coming and going all the time. The new units arriving at that time didn't even know we existed, so it was no wonder that this happened. Information didn't always filter down very well – not on these bases.

One new unit that arrived came complete with a full-blown American General, who came into the camp just generally have a look around. He found us tucked away in our corner of the camp and as usual the Fijians were singing, as they did every night. This was really pretty soothing and relaxing, as they had fantastic voices. This General was walking around the camp, and had just stumbled upon our ragtag private army posted in the farthest reaches of his camp, when he came across to ask who we were. After a lot of explaining and checking up, a great relationship struck up between us and the new army unit and he then gave us all the support we needed. In most war zones military changeovers often don't run smoothly, but this was going to be slightly different! This general didn't even know we were on his camp until he found us! Once it was established that we were one of his assets it was game on: we were now going to get every dodgy job going and this would include Iraq's forthcoming elections.

America, because of tensions, could not be seen to have

anything to do with the forthcoming elections, so we, as a private task force, were tasked to try to make things run smoothly, looking after and taking care of all the voting parties. This was a mammoth task, but, as I said, we had the respect of the local militia and, because we hadn't killed too many innocent civilians, a lot of the local people in Mosul liked us too.

As we were relaxing back in camp it was announced that the funeral of our dear departed mate (the one who'd been blown to bits when his team drove over the landmine) was to be held in the chapel of rest in Saddam's palace. This seemed quite fitting and the Fijians were going to sing for everyone. It was a very emotional service; all the services were. The Americans really went to town for us on these occasions and it was very touching how much they tried to help us with our losses. You can slag the Americans off all you want for going into Iraq, but there are a lot of excellent American people and soldiers out there. I honestly believe that some country had to take charge and the Yanks were the ones with the power to do it.

The problem with being a contractor/mercenary in Iraq is that in some of the jobs you can pick and choose, and in other jobs you can't – you don't get given a choice. You often have to go where the money is. However, once you've done the real dodgy shit the rest comes easily. It can be a very harsh learning curve but you can't moan about it.

Chapter 8
Weapons Training and Life Around the Camp

The American camp where we were based was a big place and had once been Saddam's northern HQ. There were some pretty impressive buildings on the camp and, while Saddam's people had suffered in poverty, he had lived a life of luxury, a typical tyrant. We had heard that in Baghdad they found a gold, workable, full-sized replica of Queen Elizabeth II's royal coach! We'd all actually seen it when it had been put on the back of a flatbed truck and I managed to get a picture of it. They had also seized a load of gold-plated Heckler & Koch MP5 machine guns. The massive complex contained two huge palaces surrounded by palatial buildings for Saddam's staff. Of course, since he had been overthrown, during a violent attack by the US Special Forces, the surrounding compounds had been trashed, but the buildings were remarkably undamaged. The camp was surrounded by brick walls topped with razor wire. It was very well fortified.

There was now a full complement of American troops on camp plus four private security companies. Although this place, being up north, was a lot more dangerous than the south, you had a lot more leeway. It was a nice place to be based, with a great gym, unlimited free Internet access and food that was very good. The little time off we had (when we weren't doing convoys, the mass graves, elections and route reconnaissance for the American military) was spent training – weapons-testing, first aid and tactics, mainly. It was hard to practise tactics sometimes because no two situations we encountered were ever the same. But anti-ambush drills were a big part of our training, and we also honed our weapon skills and vehicle drills the best we could until they became second nature. My main job was training the guys with the M240 and M249 light and heavy machine guns. Some of the new guys had never worked with these weapons before or even picked one up. All weapons are potentially deadly in the right hands but these weapons are *especially* so; they will blow clean through brick walls and steel plates, in fact almost anything.

We also practised vehicle drills a lot of the time. For instance, in the event of getting stuck in traffic, getting caught in an ambush or losing a vehicle due to breakdown or gunfire, everything had to be second nature to everyone. We had to try to leave nothing to chance. Every eventuality had to be considered and, if possible, catered for, so the drills had to be practised on a regular basis. After all, practice makes perfect.

Working up in the north was an amazing difference from working in Baghdad for reasons other than those I've already mentioned: in Baghdad our vehicles had to be kept immaculate and were armoured, but in the north they just had to be kept running and in one piece, if possible.

The welded steel plates along the length of the tailgate sections of the pick-ups and along the length of the door and window of the driver would stop a 7.62mm round, AK-47s being the preferred weapon of the insurgents. We'd fired at some of these plates on the range to test them out. During a contact or when we got stuck, our driver was the only one to stay in the vehicle, so we had to protect him the best we could. After the doors were taken off the truck we would weld down the tailgate to give the gunner on the back more room to manoeuvre, then armour plating was added to the back up to his waist height. Last, big wide running boards were attached to the sides of the truck so that everyone could sit facing outwards, and then all arcs of fire could be covered. The wide running boards helped to stop guys falling out when we were going round bends because you could grip or brace yourself with your feet a lot better. This did happen on one or two occasions – nothing serious, though, just a few cuts and bruises.

When we first modified these brand-spanking-new trucks it felt a bit of a waste ripping apart a £40,000 Land Cruiser or £25,000 Hilux, but it was cheaper and more effective to do what we did than spend £100,000 on armoured ones.

After our trucks were finished being modified, the team

leaders got together and decided which weapon would be mounted on the back: M240, .50-cal or M19 grenade launcher. We tried to vary these between the vehicles so as to be prepared for every eventuality.

Each of the vehicles had five men: a gunner on the back with the big guns; a driver (of course); a vehicle commander in the front passenger seat; two gunners positioned in the back seats. We were equipped with three forms of communications – HF (high-frequency), VHF and a satellite phone. We also carried some bomb-jamming equipment which was, obviously, limited to certain devices. IEDs were triggered normally by a mobile phone or something similar (all the insurgents had to do was call it and the device would go off).

The kit we had could stop some of this but not the more sophisticated devices. Another triggering method favoured by the insurgents was a command wire. This was basically a wire that ran across the ground and was actually connected to the device and could be triggered by a presser switch. All the insurgent had to do was go to his local hardware store, buy a big roll of electrical wire (preferably dark-coloured so that it was hard to see), then get hold of a battery and – hey presto! – one detonation and triggering method.

Whenever we ventured out we could carry whatever weapons we wanted – whatever was in the armoury, anyway. We had a choice: M16, M16 with 203 grenade launcher, HKG3, AK-47 and HKMP5 sub-machine-gun. Because the MP5 is a 9mm, it's not really worth a wank doing the job we were doing, so hardly anyone carried one, though some of the guys preferred to carry one instead of a pistol.

The Yanks, as you know, thought we were headcases because we had no armour and we were driving around with no doors on, but we had speed and the ability to get out of the vehicles fast, which gave us the ability to react quickly. And we had the aggression. We soon got a name and reputation for ourselves as being effective and not a company to mess with. Attacking us was a last resort for the insurgents – they knew that we had no rules of engagement against them that we would have to adhere to, and that, if one of them so much as raised a head, we'd unleash hell and blow them to pieces.

Life on camp was pretty enjoyable and was made even better for having excellent guys to work with, and we were under the command of two fantastic bosses, both of whom were former US Special Forces. When we weren't fixing up the trucks (which took a lot of time because most were full of holes from bullets and shrapnel) we were on the range.

The range we used was next to the helipad. The helipad could accommodate six choppers at any one time and was a good size, probably that of a football pitch. Sometimes we would challenge the Fijians to touch rugby – big mistake! Some of these guys were fucking awesome: 6 foot 6 and 19 stone of pure brick shithouse. Thank fuck it was only *touch* rugby. I'm far from small but there's no way I'd like to take a tackle from one of these hulks.

We lived, played and fought together until we had such a strong bond that home for me became a distant memory. Our rotation on this operation was supposed to be nine weeks work and three weeks off, but some of the lads had done thirteen months solid. I'd done five months up until now and I had almost forgotten life in the UK. I was enjoying it. This was my life now. It was like being in the mob again but more relaxed and with the added bonus of being paid a hell of a lot more. Don't get me wrong, I loved my time as a Royal Marine Commando and those guys are some of the toughest troops in the world, but this line of work was a different ball game, one at times you could become unsure about – having no backup for one.

In the Marines I was involved in three tours of Northern Ireland and the First Gulf War, but I don't think it is comparable to what today's troops are going into. No disrespect to the ground troops who did go in during the First Gulf War, but our lads are now having to fight for their lives in Afghanistan and Iraq. It's a different war these days, in my opinion. It goes back to the hardcore fighting like in the Falklands period, when troops were carrying 120 pounds of equipment and fighting for hours on end – a very tough job. And now warfare has to be conducted at very close quarters, sometimes with fixed bayonets.

Although I was here as a civilian, not fighting as such but still staring death in the face every day, we were basically working as a private army. The Americans called us mercenaries, but because we weren't officially going on combat missions we couldn't be classed as such. However, there is a loophole: if we came across American troops under effective enemy fire we could 'assist' – i.e. help them out, go on the offensive, call it whatever you will. We would fight alongside them. Sometimes we even took charge of situations. They were quite well aware of our backgrounds and knew that most of us were far more highly trained than they were. Our calmness under fire often showed this.

Does this breach the boundaries of contractor or mercenary? You make your own mind up.

If you were to ask any of the lads working up in the north or in Baghdad, I bet you would get the same answer through and through. We operated with political indifference. You don't give a shit what you are actually doing – you are just there for the money and you're doing a job that you're trained to do. Our one-hundred-man elite unit was made up of Poles, Americans, Brits, French, Irish, South Africans, Zimbabweans, Fijians and Gurkhas (Nepalese). Most companies in Iraq and Afghanistan hire Western expat soldiers as team leaders/patrol commanders; PSD (personal security detachment) teams are 90 per cent expats. Then for the troops they hire ex-Gurkhas, Fijians or Peruvians. Wages in Iraq today are not what they used to be but there is still good cash to be made. South African companies are flooding the market and wages have gone down, as low as £140 per day for an expat; the Gurkha and Fijian base rate was $50 per day and Peruvians' rate was as low as $33 per day.

A major reason a lot of these PMCs are used is that, essentially, we are civilians and civilian or company casualties don't have to be reported. If the US used their soldiers to do all of the work, (a) they would have to commit more troops and (b) more of them would die or be permanently maimed. The American government were using us as tools of war and also so that US citizens could avoid being drafted because, obviously, if this was to happen the government would become extremely unpopular, probably losing votes. No government wants this, as it could quite possibly be political suicide.

We would have a good laugh with the other companies around camp. At the end of the day, we were all in the same boat. We were there for the same thing: the rush and the money. Anyone who says different is, in my opinion, kidding themselves. I know guys who were formerly elite solders in fantastic jobs in civvy street with great money, wives and kids – a nice life – who went back to Iraq as contractors and took a wage cut to do it just for the buzz. Once a soldier, always a soldier. We'd sometimes have a drink together, moan about wages (as I said, some of the South Africans were on £4,000 a month – £140 a day – while we were on £14,000 a month), moan about the companies we were working for – just like being in the forces again but with more dosh. And, of course, it was all friendly banter.

All the expats were issued with an M9 Beretta pistol. In body-guarding situations these pistols are essential, but in this job we were doing they were pretty useless. Most of us just carried an AK-47 and put it in the footwell of the vehicle as a backup weapon, but the pistols came in handy when you were running around or walking around camp. We used to joke that this was in case we were about to be captured. If I was in a situation where I needed to use my pistol and our situation was beyond repair we would most certainly be fucked. I would shoot our team then me. Ex-forces guys reading this book will probably say 'Bullshit, what a wanker!' But once you actually see what the insurgents are capable of (and I've already given you a taste of that) you'd consider it – we had all made a pact to do just that.

I gave my pistol to my driver – his M16 was too unwieldy inside the confined space, and I always carried a spare. If there was no way out and we were certainly fucked, we would do it. You stood a lot bigger chance of getting caught or killed up here than in Baghdad. If you don't take these things into account, you shouldn't be doing the job we were doing. It was my job to make sure nothing like this would ever happen – period. However, the pistol would always remain a joke, but we all seriously knew it wasn't.

Please don't get me wrong. I think the bravest man in the world is the man who has to look after his family. But, although a lot of the lads I worked with were family men, most of these guys craved, or even needed, the adrenalin rush (and obviously the money).

For your wife or girlfriend back home, it is a daily drama of not knowing how you are or where you are; if you are going to be killed, or if you've already been killed; or what the hell is actually happening to you. Ask any partner what they would prefer. You at home on £500 a week or getting your arse shot off for £2,500 a week? I think that most partners would rather have you 'safe' at home and in one piece. This was a predicament I didn't have to face. A lot of these guys were here just to get themselves out of debt and some, as I said, were here for the buzz.

As we woke to a beautiful, crisp morning, I decided to take our brat of a dog, Kasper, for a run along the perimeter. I put my pistol in my hip holster, which I used to put on my arse because Berettas are big pistols and trying to run with one on your hip is a nightmare. The Iraqi civilians on camp and some of the troops were always trying to kill the wild dogs that used to hang around, so we sprayed the back of our dog green so that they knew she was one of ours and would not kill her. Kasper didn't mind that we'd sprayed her green, but she was still a feral little bastard.

So there I was happily jogging along with our green-arsed dog when I heard a familiar sound: the whistle of an incoming mortar. I grabbed the dog and then dived for cover; the dog then tried to bite me. We dived onto the ground, as I didn't have any cover nearby. Boom! I couldn't tell where the mortar landed but it sounded close. Then there was another. All the time that this was going on the fucking dog, which I was trying to protect, was biting the crap out of me, the little sod!

The Fijians and the Gurkhas were fond (I must admit, I was as well) of this mad little pooch so I resisted letting her go, and I put up with the nipping. It must have looked pretty hysterical. There was I, appearing to be wrestling this little yappy dog, and, though it may have looked as if I were trying to strangle her, far from it: I was doing my best to save our beloved pet. Following the third mortar strike the Americans started opening up, firing at the mortar position.

The US military have this special detection equipment set up to find the direction of incoming fire from mortars. It turned out that it was coming from a huge hotel that was situated around 200 metres from the perimeter of the camp. All of a sudden the mortaring stopped, so our green-arsed, nasty, feral but lovely puppy dog and I carried on with our run. That dog loved running, funnily enough, but the fucker kept trying to trip me up by weaving around me or cutting me up. I had to keep her on a bit of rope, which could be entertaining.

After getting laughed at for a good thirty minutes on our run because of Kasper, I arrived back at the accommodation, showered and sat down on my small throne. We'd all been permitted at some time, or maybe not, to take some furniture out of Saddam's palaces, so some of us even had chaises longues while some of the other guys had acquired gold-leaf chairs. I sat and relaxed for a little while, put on some chill-out music and fell asleep.

I woke and remembered that this morning we were doing

weapons training. The minor problem we had with this was that, while the Fijians had been trained in the M16 American assault rifle, the Gurkhas, being of different origin and having been Pakistan- or British-trained, had not been. This meant everyone was used to a different weapon and, therefore, had to be trained with the M16 (because it was only the expats who got a *choice* of weapon – everyone else had to have an M16). At the range, therefore, we didn't really have to concentrate on the Fijians' training, just the Gurkhas'. The Fijians just had to do the range and zero, test and adjust their sights. It wasn't that the Gurkhas couldn't shoot – they certainly could – just that some things were different for them with the M16.

The safety procedures employed on the range were very strict because it was on the outer edge of the helipad. If a chopper was coming in you had to stop firing immediately, unload and generally just be very careful – chopper pilots get very nervous around guns for hire because professionalism varies quite a lot through the different companies. If you accidentally hit a chopper, you and the company you're working for would be in deep shit, really deep shit. I'm not saying that you'd purposely do it, but there was always the chance of a ricochet on ranges. We always had to post a sentry who had a radio link with the American headquarters, and would inform us of any incoming aircraft.

Following the range practice that day – which went really well apart from a few minor mishaps – the standards were all pretty good. We then had to let the Fijians get some grub. The CIA had booked the range for the rest of the morning, anyway, so we had to get off. PMCs always came second in anything concerned with the US military, or US civilian intelligence agencies. We had also heard a rumour that an important VIP was coming in today, but we weren't told who. As it turned out the rest of the day was uneventful – just a bit of gym and a bit of bumming around. Pretty chilled out and no more mortars, thank fuck!

Around teatime I was coming out of the canteen, after a nice steak, when I saw two Apache attack helicopters and a Black Hawk transport helicopter coming in. I guessed this could be the VIP, as it was not normal for two Apaches to be escorting a Black Hawk – normally they fly independently of each other. The Black Hawks are also pretty well armed, so wouldn't usually need Apaches to escort or protect them. So I sat on the wall outside the citadel and waited to see who it could possibly be.

Following a short wait, a load of Triple Canopy guys came up to the building escorting ex-President Bill Clinton. Bill Clinton recognised me as a contractor because of my civilian clothes and pistol. He came up, shook my hand and said what a great job we were doing. He asked which company I was working for and I told him. He said he was hearing great stuff about us and that we had a good reputation back in Washington, DC. I didn't really give a toss, but it was kind of cool to shake the hand of an ex-president of the United States! After my brief meeting I headed back to my quarters. I was pretty knackered and soon dropped off to sleep after watching yet another crap copied DVD.

The next morning was uneventful, apart from the one game of touch rugby we had on the helipad with the Fijians – always a laugh if not knackering. Later that morning – after getting stuffed at touch rugby – my mate Malcolm came down to see me. Malcolm was CIA and his job was computers – monitoring them (basically computer spying) to see what the insurgents were up to and generally keeping an eye on things. He told me that things were hotting up and movements of the insurgents were increasing.

These CIA guys were the eyes and ears on the ground, but, to be frank, even if the information they gave us was accurate and correct, it wouldn't do us much good, because the insurgents could and did move around so efficiently and effectively. We were in a no-win situation anyway and it was purely down to us to sort ourselves out. After chatting over a coffee with Malcolm I was quite interested to know that the CIA used civilian contractors as well. They were actually permitted to recruit whomever they wanted. It was always interesting talking to him, but I'm sure he came down only for the decent coffee and cold beer we had. He was a nice guy, though.

After tea we all had a couple of beers. It was always nice to relax. It was essential to be able to let off a bit of steam. We all had a pretty early night and were settling into a nice peaceful sleep when all hell broke loose. The sound of gunfire that awoke us was immense – as if it were right outside our own doors. The noise and rate of fire was tremendous. I dived out of my bed, grabbed my M16, banged a magazine on it and legged it out of the door, still in my boxers. We'd all been given 'stand-to' positions (this was basically emergency positions in the unlikely event that the camp came under attack or was overrun).

As I came running out of my door, I came face to face with Phillipe, who had the hooch next door to mine. He didn't even have his underwear on, but was stark bollock naked. All he had was his gun. This was truly a bizarre sight and if the situation wasn't so serious I would have laughed! We said we'd cover each other while we got some sort of clothes on and chucked some body armour on. Once we'd composed ourselves from our rude awakening we got into our fire positions, which were about 10 metres from our accommodation. It sounded like a shit storm was happening just outside the perimeter wall, and, because we had no comms with the Americans, we didn't know what was going on out there. All we could see were tracer rounds going just over our heads and we could hear one hell of a racket; it was pretty scary shit.

Now we were sorted in our fire positions, Phillipe and I started laughing at what we'd just experienced – running around in the bollocky buff and boxer shorts, respectively, and armed to the teeth. But now we were prepared and in good fire positions, so if anyone came in we'd fuck 'em up good and proper. I popped a 40mm grenade into the breach of my M203 and prayed I'd maybe hit something. There was now even more firepower going down and ricocheting everywhere and the whole of our squad were legging it around in a bit of a confused state trying to establish where the best place to form a defence would be.

The next moment amazed me. All the shooting and noise stopped and a deathly quiet descended. We all, rather apprehensively, got up and gathered round for a chat. What the fuck had just happened? No one knew, so we sent one of our American guys up to the citadel (because he could get access) in the hope of finding out what had just gone down. When he came back he informed us that, as an American patrol had come out of the gate, they had driven straight into an insurgent ambush. They had encountered heavy-calibre machine-gun fire, rocket-propelled grenades, the lot. The insurgents really had it in for them. In return, the Yanks had opened up with everything they had and the noise was truly incredible! No wonder it sounded like World War Three! Pretty much all the insurgents bought it; the ones who had survived were wounded and so were arrested. No Americans were hurt or killed.

I found it quite moving sometimes watching the faces of these young American troops after they had been involved in a bad contact where they had maybe lost a mate or a lot of friends. You could practically see them age overnight, and over time their composure changed and a lot of them looked sad and homesick.

As mercenaries from different parts of the world and widely differing backgrounds, we could sometimes find it difficult to understand where each of us was coming from, but we all managed to gel eventually and we formed a great team. To this day I have fond memories of the guys I served with. There were some really great characters – most good, some bad.

Green-arsed Kasper had now become a bit of a pain in the butt. The little fucker had, when I was out, left me a nice stinking message in the middle of my floor for when I came back from the shower. It was hard to be angry with her, though, but to make matters worse for me she had been going into one of the stagnant ponds that were scattered around the base to cool down in and do a bit of swimming! She now stank to high heaven and would insist on sleeping in my room most nights. Even though the little fucker often used to nip me, we were all fond of her. It was kind of a love–hate relationship. She was, after all, a wild dog. When the green paint wore off, though, she'd always get a respray for her own protection.

Life around camp was never dull. There was always something going on. We'd now had a day or two off and managed to get some time to patch up some of the vehicles (which we had to do quite often) when a US Major came over for a chat – he was a commander in charge of the Stryker armoured personnel carriers. We all got chatting about missions that we'd been on and he started asking about Tikrit, which we used to travel through every now and then, and Tal Afar. I told him about our wheel-changing fiasco, which made him chuckle a little. I said to him that when he took his guys through there he should watch his arse, and he gave me a sly smile in return – as if saying to me, 'Don't patronise us, we're the US military, we know what we're doing.' I left it at that. If he didn't want advice on an unfamiliar hostile area so be it – more fool him. In my book any free advice is good advice. We went our separate ways and I carried on helping to fix our ravaged, bullet-riddled trucks.

Later in the day I saw the same major. I had to laugh, because he'd been shot in the arm and had it in a cast. I know that this sounds a bit cruel, but apparently, knowing best (of course!), he'd stuck his head out of the Stryker to have a look and observe a few places in this most dangerous of towns and he'd been taken out by a sniper. Poetic justice I would call it, and I have to admit to feeling a little smug about it all. Of course, it would have been no laughing matter if he had been killed, but he'd got off lightly considering his audacity, and the sniper had only winged him. He'd be OK and maybe a little wiser.

It was some of the Yank forces' tactics to try to bribe local tribal leaders with dollars in order to get some insurance, we hoped, that we wouldn't get hit or caught with an IED going through trouble spots. This was extremely cost-effective for us – if it worked – for a couple of reasons: (a) you didn't have to get a new vehicle if you were taken out and (b), more importantly, you'd have safe passage through that area. For a few bucks you could save the lives of your guys. We had good heads on our shoulders and we knew what we were doing. As always, our aim was getting from A to B in one piece.

We'd already gone through twenty-seven vehicles so far on this tour, which is a shocking number, but the job we were doing was never going to be easy. Difficult as it already was, though, things were going to get worse – far, far worse – and this was going to be a hard lesson to learn. You have to try to expect the unexpected, but there's only so much you can do.

The insurgents were now blowing up oil pipelines, trying to fuck up the country's infrastructure. It was going to be our job to prevent this if we could. I could see this getting messy, very messy. When you have a committed force of guys hell bent on trying to kill you, you could all be in deep shit. With insurgents, you can't piss around with warning shots or shouted warnings. You shoot to kill. You aim for the biggest body part. The chest area is the easiest to hit, and a strike there normally does the most damage. Unless you are extremely close, head shots are a myth unless you are a sniper in a good static position. That's why, when we'd got into the contact outside the CIA safe house (see Chapter 5), I'd tried to blow up that motherfucker who'd tried to jump over the wall with my M203 – it's a bigger weapon than my 5.56mm M16. It's a nasty business having to take someone's life, but of course it's a necessity in our line of work.

A few days after that gun battle had caught us with our pants down, the most bizarre thing happened to us. We were all relaxing when the unimaginable happened – a big chunk of the camp's perimeter wall, which was just outside our accommodation, unexpectedly fell over! I think it was purely down to structural weaknesses, not anything to do with sabotage. We were now totally open and exposed to the main highway in Mosul and in an extremely vulnerable position.

Phillipe, Dwight and I grabbed our kit and stood there guarding the 30-metre gap. What we were doing was fucking dodgy but was obviously essential not only for our safety but for the safety of the whole camp – who knew what might happen? So there we stood waiting for the might of the American military to turn up and relieve us and take charge. We got into the best cover we could manage, and then we spent a very nervous night on tenterhooks. We were jumping at every shadow and noise and frantically scanning the darkness looking for any movement. It was a safety-catches-off situation.

The darkness was impenetrable to the naked eye, and we didn't have the benefit of the hi-tech night-vision goggles that the Yanks had. We did have some provided to us but they weren't of very good quality and we felt they didn't help us at all. We didn't have night sights on our weapons, either. Many hours later, and with our nerves stretched to breaking point, the Americans finally turned up to relieve us. We thankfully returned to our hooches to get some well-deserved sleep. We'd been up for hours, with no backup, and we were knackered.

The next morning all we had was an airport run to do, just run-of-the-mill stuff but always an arse twitcher, since any trip was dangerous here. One of our guys was going on leave and it's not as if you could just call a cab to run him across town. It was always a case of running the gauntlet through Mosul – never a dull moment.

It was always nice when you arrived at the airport. There was a great American duty-free shop. You could even order a Harley-Davidson motorcycle or buy a car if you wanted, and all at great discount prices. These could be delivered anywhere in the world. Also, you could get some great knock-off American kit: extra magazines for our weapons and general 'Gucci' kit ('Gucci' is a term we used in the mob to describe any nice designer gear or special kit). We could even blag extra ammo from the store that was situated around the back of the PX (Post Exchange). It was all good stuff.

In northern Iraq, if there was a chance to grab a bargain or, even better, get something for free, you grabbed it! You never knew when anything might come in handy – like the American military-issue body armour (which most of us were now wearing), which was shit hot. It was nice and snug, well fitting and comfortable with the added bonus of giving loads more protection. Even the sides of these jackets with no plates in could stop a 9mm round. The ones we were issued with could do all of this but the American vests fitted better. And, as we've seen, you could attach your kit to them, such as ammo pouches, which meant you could do away with wearing webbing vests. It all made for a better system to wear, and was more effective to run around in if you had to debus.

Chapter 9

On Leave

We'd come through the end of summer in northern Iraq now and you could tell, because the temperature had dropped dramatically. In the south it stays pretty warm all year round but in the north it gets very cold (it can go well below freezing), and it snows.

(After the First Gulf War, when I was still a Royal Marines Commando, one of our main jobs was to force the pockets of the elite Republican Guard out of northern Iraq and repatriate the Kurdish people, who had been driven up into the mountains. When we got off the choppers in the valleys it was around 35°C, but we had all our winter gear on and we were roasting; but up in the mountains it was always freezing with snow on the peaks. This is the area where the poor Kurds were forced to live.)

So all the gear we were wearing now had to change. We exchanged our desert boots for Gore-Tex-lined ones. We had to get insulated work jackets, gloves, woolly hats, etc.

The mornings were now freezing, so, instead of the usual warm stroll over to the showers, it was now a sprint in your towel. There would be steam pouring out of the shower block. In fact, it was so unpleasant running around camp in a towel that during one mission up into Kurdistan we all bought ourselves dressing gowns to try to combat that early-morning chill.

Since there were only twenty-eight or so expats working on this project, we obviously couldn't take leave all at once, so the boss asked us to put in leave requests. We had to try to stagger it so that only a couple of guys were on leave at any one time. To tell you the truth, unbelievable though it sounds, most of us were happy just to stay put. We were all earning around £14,000 a month and happy just letting the money come in and doing a job we all enjoyed. The fact that you're putting your life on the line every day doesn't enter into it. Obviously, it crosses your mind, but you never think anything will ever happen to you, always the other poor fucker.

Going on leave for some of the guys wasn't straightforward at all. We had a few guys from Zimbabwe and if, on their arrival back in their own country, it was found out that they'd been working in Iraq they would be banged up and tortured for being mercenaries! However, because private companies controlled the airports in Iraq, there were no stamps in our passports and in Kuwait we could travel on our American forces ID cards – so, again, no stamps. These Zimbabwean guys had to be so careful. On our ID card we were given the civvy equivalent of a colonel. This wasn't to give us any authority; rather, it was in the event of our getting injured or killed, since it would speed up the process of getting flown to Germany, where the main American hospital was. For most of us going on leave, it was a pretty simple process. All we had to do was get to the airport in Mosul, then back through Kuwait, on to Amsterdam and then back into the UK, normally Heathrow.

It was early November and I'd packed the stuff I was going to take home. That wasn't much, just pants and socks and other clothes. I went to the armoury and handed in my weapons and ammo but I took my optical sight off, just in case it got 'borrowed'. I'm not for one minute saying that anyone would have nicked it. It's just that with an operation this size things can and do get lost. After handing in all that was necessary I got a lift up to the office from one of the Fijians. At least for this leave I would have a travelling partner: Phillipe was flying as far as Amsterdam with me. The wait-up at the ops room was boring as hell. Once I had my going-home head on that was it – I wanted to get going and get home.

Within about an hour we were off. I chucked my stuff in the back of the truck and gave the dog a hug; the little fucker tried to nip me again! Still wild at heart. How anyone could actually love this dog was beyond me, but we did. I sat in the middle in the back seat of the truck. It felt strange to be in someone else's hands as I was used to being in control. I had been given a standard M16 for the ride to the airport but if anything happened on the way there wouldn't be a lot that I could do unless we debussed. I just wanted to be on that BA flight with a beer in my hand, chilling out and watching a movie as soon as possible.

After the normal mad dash across town, we arrived at the airport. I grabbed my gear out of the back and met up with Phillipe, and we hugged all the guys and said our goodbyes. I wondered which faces would be missing when I got back. I hoped it wasn't many – it was a sobering thought. In that instant, I didn't want to leave, didn't want to be left out, wanted to be there with them when the shit went down – mad thoughts, but very real. We were a team, we'd built up a bond, a strong one at that. It felt as if these guys had now become my family and I felt as if I were abandoning them, leaving my 'family' to face all that shit alone.

I walked to passenger processing with Phillipe. We didn't say a word to each other and I knew that he was probably feeling exactly the same as I was. We decided to dump our stuff and go to a nice restaurant. They had four. The Yanks had really got their shit together when it came to this sort of thing. We dumped our gear and headed for the supermarket and cafés. We could see our convoy heading out of the gate – probably to get the Fijians back in time for more food! I quietly wished them Godspeed under my breath.

After a quick look around the supermarket, I bought a couple of presents for mates: a few Yank Army T-shirts, a couple of Gerber knives, stuff like that. Time was getting on, so we grabbed some food and sat and waited. We managed to get ourselves on a quicker flight, which was a good result, because it meant we could spend a longer time in Kuwait, which is a far nicer place to be stuck in than Mosul.

The transit accommodation at Mosul was horrible: it consisted of a plastic mattress and that was it, no sheets, blankets, no pillows, nothing. So it was far more pleasant to sit in the TV lounge (this was open twenty-four hours and showed the latest films available). I bought myself a tea then sat down with Phillipe discussing what we were going to get up to on leave. We were due to fly out on a C-130 Hercules at around 19.00. Just then the flight sergeant came in and shouted out our names. We picked up our gear and put on our body armour and helmets and got into the transport to take us to the plane. As we trundled across the runway I wondered whether I would ever see this place again or remain in the UK. I soon snapped out of my daze and knew damn well that I would be coming back. Nearing the plane I could see a load of American soldiers at the tail, obviously going on some R 'n' R as well. They all looked pretty cheery. Some of these poor bastards hadn't been home for nearly a year, some even longer.

After we were seated on the plane, I closed my eyes and tried to get some sleep – I was asleep in a few minutes and soon I was woken up by the landing gear coming down. Next thing, we touched down in Kuwait. The Yanks all gave a big cheer. The airport for the military is huge and we found out, as the plane was unloaded, that our bags had been mislaid. Great! Then, even better, we couldn't find our transport!

Phillipe and I went to find the processing part of the place and bumped into two guys we knew. They'd got in here earlier but were still waiting to be picked up. We made a few calls and found out that, to cap it all, our lift hadn't turned up because we'd been forgotten! I spoke to our man in Kuwait City and he told us to sit tight!

I still couldn't get over the sheer size of the military airport. I just put my IPod on and found a comfy spot. Around three hours passed, then someone kicked my foot. I looked up and there was a smiling Gurkha. 'You ready to go, Mr Pete?' I motioned to the others to grab their stuff and we all got into an American SUV that the Gurkha was driving.

Travelling through the airport on the way out, I saw a familiar face. I wound down my window and called out, 'Will!' He looked around and shouted, 'All right, mate!' But we didn't stop and I've never seen him since! I hadn't seen Will in nearly ten years, not since I had served with him in the Royal Marine Commandos. We'd done a few tours of Northern Ireland and had been through some scrapes together. There are approximately fifty-thousand contractors in Iraq, so it is inevitable that you will bump into someone you've served with in the past somewhere along the line.

After catching a few z's and an hour's drive, we got to the office. The sun was just rising and I witnessed a beautiful sunrise. We were welcomed at the office by Tom, who apologised for the cock-up but insisted it was nothing to do with him. Rather it had been the Mosul end that was responsible for the breakdown of communications. All of us were starving, so in an instant we were out of the door and walking along the beach towards the restaurant. The weather in Kuwait was pretty warm, about 25°C. It made a nice change from the wet and windy Iraq we'd just left. After a delicious breakfast and a good deal of looking at the lovely waitresses, we headed back to the office with a little regret – those chicks were hot, really great eye candy, but I figured that, as I'm an ugly bastard, I wouldn't stand a chance.

Tom was looking a bit sombre when we arrived back. 'Did any of you know John Barker from Baghdad?' he asked.

'Yeah,' I said, 'I do. I worked with him for a few months. He's a good mate, why?'

'Got some terrible news, Pete,' he said.

As soon as the words had left his mouth I knew that John was dead. Doing the job we did, if someone talked of 'something terrible', we just knew someone had been killed. John had been an ex-Royal Marine Commando, then he'd joined the Metropolitan Police and ended up in its elite SO19 firearms team. When he had left that job he came out to Baghdad and worked with us.

From what we could gather, John had been working on Checkpoint 1 at Baghdad International Airport (this was the main entrance to the airport). There had been a queue

171

of cars waiting to get in. John was head of the security and the search team and had approached a car that had one male occupant in it. John had obviously sensed the guy was dodgy and he got down into a firing position and was asking the guy to get out of the car when the guy triggered his suicide bomb.

John didn't stand a chance. He was blown apart, apparently killed instantly. John's death was a shock to me and everyone who knew him. We all talked about it for a while, especially Phillipe, who had also worked with him. John was a lovely man, God bless him. Another secret death statistic in the volatile country of Iraq.

We were due out of Kuwait on the evening flight. This was due to get us into Amsterdam during the early morning. We left all our body armour and helmets in the office, did our last-minute emails to friends and family and were off to the airport. At the terminal we went through all the searches, which are the standard for all civilian travellers, but because of our Yank IDs we didn't have to take our shoes off and, as was common practice, we got through customs pretty quickly. I must admit now, I was really looking forward to getting home, seeing my family and my mates, going out for some nice food, some beers – just doing normal stuff. I realised how alienated I'd made myself in Iraq, how I'd shut out the outside world. I'd made Iraq my be-all and end-all, and now it was time to get back to normal and reality, for a while at least.

We started to get on the plane. I'd chosen a window seat.

Even today I enjoy looking out of the window when flying just as I did when I was a kid. Soon we had taken off. I was seated next to Phillipe. The seat-belt sign went off and the air stewardesses came round. One lady mentioned that she thought we were soldiers on our way back from Iraq. We just replied that we worked there, and from that moment on we got a lot of attention. I ended up with six free bottles of wine and Phillipe had more free Heineken than he could drink – but we both did our best, obviously. We both ended up sleeping more than anything else, though, and it wasn't long before we were touching down in Amsterdam.

Once we were in the terminal, Phillipe and I said our goodbyes to the other two guys and went for a walk around Schiphol. I tried my best to get Phillipe to come back to my house in the West Country for a few days before he went back to France, but he had to get home. I had a quick browse around the airport, but was soon on a plane back to Heathrow. I'd called a mate of mine and asked if he could pick me up from the bus station back in the West Country, but he insisted on coming to Heathrow to get me, which was kind.

As the plane touched down at Heathrow, I was again looking out of the window and could see that it was pissing down! I got off the plane and went through customs as fast as possible. I was soon stood outside the terminal in the pouring rain. My mate Rodders was waiting for me. I hadn't seen him for months. We gave each other a hug and then I jumped into his car. We chatted nonstop all the way home. It was hard trying to explain what I'd been doing, so I kept talk of Iraq to a minimum. Instead I just caught up with all the gossip from back home. It made me realise how life goes on and how much I had missed out on while I had been away – it made me feel more than a bit homesick.

Nothing seemed to have changed and Rod had been looking after my motorbike, a Ducati 916; I love that bike, but it's got me into trouble sometimes.

Before going to Iraq I had decided it was going to be a hell of a long time before I rode my motorbike again, if ever, because there was a very real possibility I might never have returned. It could be my last chance for a burn. So one morning I jumped on my 916 and went for a blast. I'd met up with a few friends and we headed for Monmouth in Wales. Most of my mates were riding Suzuki GSXRs and Yamaha R1s, but I guess there's no accounting for individual taste! There are some great twisty fast roads on the way and that day we were maybe breaking a speed limit or two.

I was just slowing down to come through a small village when I saw the dreaded blue lights behind. I pulled over, got off my bike and took off my helmet. 'Good morning, sir. Do you know why I've pulled you over?' the officer asked.

'Well it's probably not to compliment me on my riding,' I replied. The copper gave a chuckle and asked me to get in the car. He showed me a reading of 92 m.p.h. in a 60 m.p.h. zone and promptly gave me a ticket. No bollocking, no nothing, just gave me the ticket and sent me on my way.

Well, with all the rush and commotion of shipping out to Iraq I'd totally forgotten about this speeding ticket I'd been given and I hadn't informed the police that I couldn't make the court date. What a fuck-up! I've got a mate, whom I used to play rugby with, who is a copper back home, and he had told my mate Rodders that I now had a warrant out for my arrest. Fuck! Now I was in the shit!

When we arrived home I had nowhere to stay after my split with my ex, so Rodders said I could have his spare room at his house. We'd made the decision that she was going to buy me out of the house, so I was effectively homeless. I wasn't bothered by this, though, because in less than three weeks I'd be back in Iraq. I would worry about somewhere to live when I got back the next time – if I got back. I had enough dosh to set myself up for now. I unpacked my small selection of clothing, then went for a walk into town. I said hi to a few familiar faces, then went for a pint in the local. It felt as if I'd never been away. I just sat there and mulled over what an absurd experience I'd just been through.

Over the next few days I did a bit of cycling through the local woods on my mountain bike, then decided to go to the cop shop to sort my motorbike thing out. The copper on the desk was a sound bloke and pretty understanding about the situation I had unfortunately found myself in. He promptly arrested me, then bailed me to appear in front of Swansea Magistrates' Court at a later date. I explained that I would be away again in just under three weeks and he said he would try to get me a court date within my leave period. I was happy that I wasn't going to jail and went back to Rodders's house and booked a rail ticket to go up north to see my parents. I'd not seen them for such a long time.

Now my mum and dad are really relaxed, chilled-out people, and it takes a lot to wind them up; and to put up with a son like me made them very special people in my eyes! I'd lied to start with about Iraq and I'm sure they understood why I'd done that. Mum was crapping herself, and I'm positive my old man was as well, but he just doesn't show it. I was soon in York and caught a taxi to my parents' place, but on the way I decided to stop at my sister's. She was glad to see me and it was pretty emotional. She came with me to my parents' and we had a great night in. I tried to keep the conversation away from Iraq.

I stayed a week in York, then decided it was time to get back down south. Although I love my parents dearly, a week of just sitting around the house doing nothing can wear a bit thin – especially when you've got only about eighteen days left. So the next morning my old man said he'd drop me at the railway station because he had to drop my mum at Tesco, where she worked. As we pulled up at the supermarket, I got out and gave my mum a hug. She went to pieces, pleading with me not to go back. She was bawling her eyes out. I felt like the worst son in the world. I'd never seen my mum in this sort of state before. After my tearful goodbye, Dad dropped me at York railway station. Then, after another tearful goodbye – with my dad this time – I jumped on my train back down south.

The evening I arrived back, a mate of mine, Mick, asked if I'd like to go to Alton Towers with him, his wife and kids. I thought it would be a laugh, so the next morning I got picked up around 06.00. Mick was a good mate from ages back. His wife was lovely and the kids (boys aged eleven and nine) were great. It took us about four hours to get there from Bristol. Once there we got the tickets and then there was no messing. The kids were off and running with me in tow!

My plan was to chat with Mick and his missus all day, chill out, go for a walk, have a nice lunch, a few beers, you get the picture – a nice day. The kids were having none of it. I was dragged off to the Pirate Ship. This didn't look too bad, and it wasn't. Then on we went to the Black Hole. I went – I didn't have a choice! – but you can't see anything, so this ride wasn't so bad, either. I'd never been to Alton Towers before, so I'd never seen rollercoasters like this. We came to one called the Corkscrew and I was challenged to ride it – it wasn't even 11.00 yet. I climbed aboard with nervous laughter, leaving Mick and his missus on the side watching.

I was strapped in and we were off. Fuck me backwards! I shat myself. I was so scared, I couldn't even scream. It was hell. When we stopped I just sat there in silence. I thought they were going to have to pry my vicelike grip off the bars! Next came the Thunder Looper. These kids just wouldn't let up. There was no escape! I was getting dragged around everything, like it or not. Trembling and cursing under my breath, I got on, bricking it again. Whoosh! *'Aaaaaarrrgh!'* Upside down we went. *'Noooo!'* I screamed – it was terrifying. What a wuss I was being!

By lunch my nerves were shot and I was wandering around in silence, crapping myself at the thought of more rides. Ironic, really: the previous week I'd been in the most dangerous country in the world dodging bullets and bombs and I had felt good. Now two little kids had reduced me to a complete nervous wreck.

We sat down for lunch and all of us looked around for a bar. A couple of shots of Dutch courage did nothing for me. In fact, I think it made me worse. Now, not only was I still shit scared but, to cap it all, off I was now feeling more than a little nauseous.

Next was Nemesis. My nerves were still shot to pieces from the earlier experiences, and I'm sure that the attendant had to guide me to my seat a little. I'm not sure, but I think I was shaking. I was bad, but at least I didn't have any tears running down my legs – well not so far, anyway! That was the last ride I went on and the last time I will go to Alton Towers. I felt ill and vowed never to go again. It's strange: I've done hundreds of free-fall parachute jumps and have done six base jumps, but these roller coasters! Fuck that! You can keep them. They totally scare the shit out of me.

After getting back from Alton Towers, I went around to my ex's to see about getting my stuff. She was pleased to see me but not overecstatic. I decided to try to play it as nice as I could. After all, we'd been together for five years, but the relationship had run its course. She also got tearful when I said I was going back. Although we were now split up, she still had strong feelings for me, but I left on good terms and we still keep in touch to this day.

My leave time was passing quickly, and the date of my court appearance was approaching. But that was not just yet. As I was walking up to Rodders's house one day, with about a week left of my stay, I stopped for a pint in the local. As I was entering the boozer my mobile went off. It was a call from one of our guys in Iraq. What I was told next made me down a double vodka. Sixteen of the Gurkhas I'd worked with in Iraq had been killed by an RPG fired into their compound in Baghdad in the Green Zone. Later, I was to look at the pictures he sent me by email. It looked awful. The rocket had exploded and this had caused a big fire. The accommodation huts were just a burned-out mess. The Gurkhas who hadn't been killed by the RPG had probably burned to death, unable to get out of their huts. I could, unfortunately, easily imagine what a truly horrific death that must have been.

Not long after this incident, eight Nepalese security guys (nothing to do with us) were kidnapped by the insurgents and later beheaded. This was enough for the Nepalese government, and they put a ban on any of their nationals going to work in Iraq. This was a big blow to all the security companies working in the country, because a lot, if not most, of their troops came from Nepal and were ex-Gurkhas.

Security companies had to do something drastic to avoid the ban, so basically what they started to do was bounce the Nepalese troops through varying different countries first, to camouflage their movements, then on to Kuwait. Once these companies got these guys there, they were there to stay. The guys didn't get leave, anyway. Most had to do at least a year before returning home.

The weekend, anyway, was a bit of a mess. It was the last one of my leave, and I'd not really been out on a drinking session with my friends since I'd got back. It wasn't a mental drinking frenzy that we went on, and a lot of my mates brought their partners, including my mate Phil, who, in his case, brought his boyfriend along. It was a great day and night.

The wife of one of my mates said I was brave for working in Iraq. I said to her, 'Look, I'm not over there for queen and country. Fuck that. I was there for my mates and money — cold hard cash. I'm not brave. Stupid, maybe, but not brave.' I hope I didn't offend her. Nobody spoke to me about Iraq much, which suited me fine. I think they all knew that I wouldn't want to talk about it. I did get the occasional arsehole trying to give me shit for being an 'invader'. I think they thought I was in the military. I just tried to ignore them. We were having a great night and the beer was flowing freely. Everyone had a right laugh.

I'd done a lot of parachuting when in the forces and quite a lot of civilian free fall also. Now my brother-in-law, Mark, used to be in the Dangerous Sports Club way back in the 1980s, so he had encouraged me into the sport of base jumping. He reasoned that, as I'd done so many freefall jumps in the past, I would be ready to have a go at it. So one night we'd driven over to Chepstow and found this massive electricity pylon. We'd climbed up the 550 feet of ladders and I had jumped off. What a laugh it was and a big adrenalin rush and, as everything went well, I couldn't get the big stupid grin off my face for hours.

So, now that I was back on leave, Mark challenged me to do another one. Call me stupid but I was well up for it. It would be only my second base jump, but the first one had been so much fun that I was eager to have another go.

That second base jump has to be one of the most memorable (and probably stupid) things I've ever done. Mark had challenged me to jump off Bristol's Clifton Suspension Bridge. We went up to Bristol to do a recce and, once standing on it, I kept asking Mark if he was sure it was high enough. He was very blasé about it and told me that he'd jumped off it about a dozen times. I remained a bit doubtful but, in the face of a bit of good-natured ribbing, I decided that, if he could do it, I certainly could. Mark reckoned the best time to do it and not get caught was a Sunday morning. So we decided to do it that weekend.

What we did next was equally stupid. We went to the pub on the Saturday afternoon – it was a lovely sunny day and not really that cold for November, and while sat in the beer garden, drinking beer, we packed the parachute for the next day.

Sunday morning came and Mark and Rodders picked me up at 07.00, which meant that I'd be jumping at around 08.00. Another mate in another car was going to be waiting for me on the Portway (the main road running below the bridge) to pick me up when I'd landed and enable us to get away before the police arrived to arrest us. I'd never actually met this guy (he was a friend of a friend) but he had volunteered to pick me up because he'd never seen a base jump before and was keen to see one.

On the way up to the bridge, Mark was giving a briefing about my jump when I decided that if I was going to do such a ridiculous thing, I might as well do it naked – in for a penny, in for a pound. Mark thought I was fucking nuts and said so. So there I was, getting my kit off in the back of Rodders's motor while trying my best not to be seen by passing cars. I was also trying to don my parachute as inconspicuously as I could. What a fucking laugh! As we approached the bridge I had to lie down as low as possible to avoid being spotted as we went through the toll booths. Rodders paid the 25p toll while I was lying in the back seriously reconsidering the whole naked thing. After all, a naked man in a parachute might draw a bit of attention.

Mark announced that he had to check the wind speed and direction – fucking great! I didn't even know where I was going to land. I felt like putting my kit back on and going home and forgetting about it. I was now bricking it and it didn't seem like such a good idea after all, but I've never been one to back down from a challenge, so, taking a deep breath, I started to go through my pre-jump checks. The plan was to land just beside the Portway on a small patch of grass. Mark suggested that maybe I should put my trainers back on because it could be a bit rough on my feet. I agreed – I really didn't want to wreck my feet.

We'd got through the tolls and screamed to a halt at my jumping point in the middle of the bridge. I scrambled out the car with Mark, just as a male jogger ran past. I said good morning and he nearly fell over, so gobsmacked was he. Obviously, a naked man with a parachute on is not something you see every day. We had to be quick, because the Clifton Suspension Bridge is a notorious suicide spot, which means that it's covered with CCTV cameras and has anti-suicide barriers to put off at least the half-hearted attempts.

Mark gave me a leg up over the wires but I still managed to catch my ball bag on the wire – which hurt like hell. I was wondering now if this was possibly the most stupid stunt I'd ever pulled in my life (with hindsight, I think it probably was). However I was up there now and ready for the off. I gave my tackle a loving rub and got ready to jump. Mark (who was standing behind me and who still denies admiring my arse) did some double checks on my chute. Everything was OK. We then saw the bridge security running towards us – it was a case of now or never.

I jumped out and arched my back to get as stable as I could very fast. After a couple of seconds of freefall I threw my drogue parachute (this is a small parachute designed to inflate, then drag your main parachute out). As soon as I'd deployed my drogue, out came my main canopy, which opened with a thwack, but I was still heading to earth at an alarming rate. My parachute was a seven-cell (this means that it has seven air pockets that need to be inflated to operate efficiently). I looked up quickly and saw that only five of the cells had opened this time and I was falling a lot more rapidly than I'd hoped, and I was also losing my steering. This was great: bollock naked (regretting that now) and with a duff parachute.

Well I totally fucked it down and within seconds I knew I was going to miss my landing target. I ended up splatting down in the estuary itself, waist deep in its stinking mud. I grabbed at the parachute and hauled it in towards me and struggled to get out of the mud. I scrambled and crawled and eventually managed to climb out of the mud and over the rail and up onto the road. I was feeling an immense sense of relief that I'd made it down and not been killed or even hurt myself, when I noticed that several cars had stopped. I think I would have stopped, too, if I had seen a person parachuting off that bridge – and there were now several carloads of people gawping at me, covered almost head to toe in mud. The only advantage of landing in the mud was that at least I wasn't really naked any more.

As I staggered up onto the main road, trying not to notice

Above: Perimeter security – guarding the elections.

Below: The Fijians. Like the Gurkhas, a bloody tough lot.

Top left: An encounter with another IED – thankfully no-one was hurt.

Top right: This truck was hit by an RPG. Unbelievably, the team sustained only minor injuries.

Above: Mick and one of the Gurkhas after an IED and firefight. The Gurkha was hit by a round in the neck and Mick was hit by shrapnel.

Right: This is Mick's neck after the contact. The shrapnel missed his artery by 2mm.

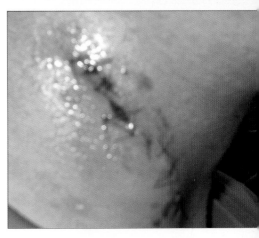

Top left: Entering the outskirts of Tikrit, a very unsettling place to be.

Top right: A convoy of 85 fuel tankers. Our task was to escort them through the centre of Mosul, no mean feat.

Middle left: One of the mine clearance vehicles we used on the mass graves mission.

Middle right: One of the mass graves.

Bottom left: A US General awarding us our civillian medals!

Bottom right: Me and the lads messing about over Christmas!

Above: All the brave Gurkhas.

Below: When the job wound down we had to hand in our hardware – and there was a hell of a lot of it.

all those people gawping at me, but also looking around for my getaway driver, I spotted the car and, carrying my parachute, ran over to him. I was a couple of yards from the car when I stopped, horror-struck. Oh, no! The guy had brought his wife and kids with him to watch. So there I was, parachute in hands, totally naked and covered in mud – I'd definitely been in better situations. I frantically covered myself up with my parachute while this wife of a friend of a friend was screeching, 'He's not getting in the car like that!' They managed to find some bin liners to cover the seats and I got in with the parachute wrapped around me feeling badly self-conscious. I sat down next to the kids, who were round-eyed and fascinated by it all. I smiled nervously and said hello to them.

Once I was in the car we sped away from the scene hoping the police wouldn't come and catch us. We shot down the M5 southwards and it wasn't long before we were home. It was now only about 08.45 and, as we pulled up, I thanked my new friend and apologised again to his missus and kids. If I'd known that they were going to be there I would never have jumped in the buff, but hopefully my parachute had covered most of my embarrassment.

As I legged it out of the car carrying all my shit with me, it dawned on me that I'd left my house keys in my jeans, which I'd left in Rodders's Audi. So there I was, naked and carrying a parachute outside Rodders's house, on a Sunday morning and hoping and praying that none of the neighbours were up. Rodders's car wasn't back and, after

I'd pounded the door for several minutes, Rodders's wife answered holding a copy of the *News of the World*. Now this was fucking amazing. Most of my mates are used to seeing me do crazy shit but she didn't even bat an eyelid when she saw me. All she said was, 'Good night, was it, Pete?' and let me in. I just walked straight past her through the house and put the parachute rig on the washing line and turned on the hose to wash it down. After a while I hid behind my parachute and I turned the hose on myself in an effort to get off most of the mud, which had started to dry and crack on my skin. God, it was freezing, but I stayed under the jet until I'd managed to get most of it off, and then ran inside to jump under a hot shower.

After my nice hot shower and some breakfast I decided that, since it was my last weekend of freedom, I should really spend some more time in the pub. I rang up Rodders to see where he was and arranged to meet him at the local for lunch. We spent the afternoon going over my jump in great detail and with much laughter. Mark turned up later looking a bit sheepish, since he'd packed the parachute for me, and he kept apologising about its not having opened fully – he swore it had never happened to him before. Oh well, I'd survived it, that was the main thing, and he had packed it when we'd both been drinking.

Monday morning came and I rang up and spoke to the lawyer who was representing me in my court case. The Crown Prosecution Service were doing me for no licence, no insurance and failing to turn up in court. Well there would be no problem with licence and insurance – I had those. It was just the failure to turn up at court that was the problem. I had a quiet night and left early for Swansea Magistrates' Court. I was up before the magistrates at 11.00. I just hoped this little escapade wouldn't affect my going back to Iraq or get me banned from driving. I nailed it to court at breakneck speed on my bike, yet again breaking the speed limit – a bit naughty I know, but I was late. I met my brief outside and he didn't think there would be too much of a problem. I had a rock-solid reason for not being able to turn up. What the hell – footballers do it all the time!

At 11.30 I was called. I went through all the bullshit that had happened and told them I'd been in Iraq and that was why I had missed the previous court case. All the magistrates looked at me incredulously. They all wanted to know what I'd been up to. So I gave a sob story about having to come home because of all the danger. Next thing, wham, bam, thank you, ma'am – three penalty points and a £100 fine. I was more than happy with that. All the magistrates wished me luck and I left the court looking as sheepish as I could.

As soon as I was home I checked my emails, then rang the office at the HQ in London to check my travel arrangements for going back. To my shock, I was to be travelling back on the Wednesday, only two days away! I started ringing around and saying my goodbyes, as I'd not got a lot of time left. A few friends had offered to take me to the coach station. I went down to the town centre to get some last-minute shopping. I wasn't actually looking forward to going back. Don't know why. But I was sure it would pass once I was on my way. When I was working in Iraq I honestly believed nothing would happen to me. However, the more I thought about it now that I was back in the UK, the more I realised that there was a very real chance of serious injury or death. It's a humbling, sobering thought.

I went into my local to say goodbye, had a pint, then went home to sort my shit out, not that I had a lot to pack.

Wednesday morning came. I grabbed my bag and got a mate of mine, who drives a taxi, to take me to the bus station, then a coach to Heathrow. I was feeling pretty low and wondering whether it was really worth it. Once you'd got back into reality land you realised what you'd experienced, and it was sometimes tough to go back to Iraq. I moped around the terminal until my flight to Amsterdam was ready, then I boarded. Soon I got my work head on and started to wonder what – apart from the sixteen Gurkhas killed by the RPG – would be different when I got back. I hoped no one else had been injured, or worse.

We soon touched down in Amsterdam. I found out which terminal I had to get to and then I was off. Amsterdam Airport at Schiphol is so massive that it can take about twenty-five minutes to get between gates, so it's worth checking your connecting terminal as soon as you get off your plane. I made my way to the departure gate before I checked the monitors again and saw, to my horror, that my connecting flight to Kuwait had been cancelled because of fog. I made enquiries at the desk but the staff there were unable to say when the airport would reopen, since nobody could predict when the fog would clear. I realised that I had to find a hotel and find one fast. Given the size of the airport and the sheer number of people it can contain, if all the flights were cancelled the hotels were going to be chock-a-block with thousands of people trying to get rooms for the night.

I had another concern as well: I had to try to get in touch with work and let them know that I was actually on my way back but was stuck at the airport. I eventually managed to find out that my flight had been rescheduled for 07.00 the next day. This was obviously going to screw up the travel arrangements from Kuwait, but there was nothing I could do; it was out of my hands. I still had to let the company know but at least I had the new flight times to tell them now. I managed to get in touch with them eventually and explained the situation. To my relief they said that it would be no problem and that they would sort out new travel arrangements for me.

I did have one bit of luck, though: when I arrived at the airport hotel, I found that, because I was classed as a frequent flyer, I could get an executive suite for only £110. I gratefully took the room, which, I've got to tell you, was pretty amazing. I turned on the telly but couldn't find anything that I wanted to watch. I was feeling restless and a bit bored, so I thought, What do you do when you're stuck in Amsterdam on your own? Answer: call a hooker. After all, I reasoned, it wasn't as if I would be betraying anyone, as I was single. I discovered that the hotel offers a great service: it has photo albums of hookers that are sent up to your room so you can pick the one you fancy – what a great country! I made my selection from the photograph and sat down on the end of the bed feeling a little guilty (for all of about two minutes if I'm honest).

After only about five minutes there was a knock on the door. That was quick, I thought, and opened the door. I couldn't fucking believe it. It was Phillipe. Not really the kind of shag I'd had in mind but it was nice to see him. I invited him in, curious about how he'd found me. Turns out that he had been due to catch the same flight as I was on (funny, I hadn't seen him at the airport, but, as I said, it was a big place). So, as he was stuck also, he'd checked into the same hotel under our company name and he'd asked the receptionist if anyone else from the company had checked in and had been given my room number. I got him a drink from the minibar and told him that I was on for a shag. I asked him if he wanted second go. Not to worry, I said, I was paying, but I was going first unless, of course, she was up for a threesome.

Phillipe was a bit straight and serious and politely declined. I figured he probably didn't want to see my mush staring back at him while he was trying to shag. No problem there, but he is far better-looking than I am (though I realise I have a bit of complex about my appearance). Phillipe downed his drink and said he'd see me at breakfast and left.

Barely five minutes after Phillipe had left, there was another knock at the door. I opened it and in front of me was a goddess (far better-looking than her photo had made her appear). I thought that she was definitely worth £70. I invited her in and introduced myself; she introduced herself as Michelle. She dumped her bag on the bed and sat down on the nightstand. She picked up her bag and started rummaging around in it, then she looked up at me and asked if I minded if she did a line of coke. Now I don't even smoke fags, so I wasn't up for it myself, but she was gorgeous and, if it relaxed her, what the fuck? Go for it.

She chopped herself a line up and snorted it quickly. I honestly think she was new to this game because she seemed really nervous – but maybe it was my ugly mug making her so jumpy. I hadn't been laid for months and thought that it would probably be over very quickly, so I didn't think she needed to worry. She picked up her bag again and found some condoms and handed one to me, then she stripped down to her underwear and looked at me expectantly. I don't think I've ever got my clothes off so quickly in my life.

We got down to business and after only about five minutes it was all over. It was probably the fastest £70 she's ever made, but I tell you what: from my point of view it was the best money I'd ever spent and definitely worth every euro. While I was still lying happily on the bed she got up and dressed herself again and after counting out her money she left. I rolled over and went to sleep.

The next morning I woke up with a big smile. I rolled over and checked the time. Shit! It was already nearly 06.00 and my flight was due to take off in little over an hour. I jumped out of bed in a panic and dragged on my clothes. I had to get over to the airport damn quick, but what I really wanted to do was get Michelle back to fuck my brains out. I even briefly considered it – it wasn't as though I was short of cash. I indulged the fantasy for a minute or so, then thought I'd best be off. I decided that I could always give the goddess a call on my way back home next time – if I made it, that is. I picked up my bags and left my room. I stopped by the restaurant but Phillipe wasn't in there. I guessed that he had already left for the airport. I grabbed a roll of bread and legged it.

I practically sprinted through the terminal looking for my departure gate. I made it in time and I was soon boarding my plane to Kuwait. I looked around and spotted Phillipe sitting about ten rows behind my seat. I gave him a little wave and settled down. I dozed off pretty fast after watching a movie. I woke up and asked for a glass of water and soon the 'Fasten Seat Belt' sign came on and we were touching down.

There was the normal bag search once we got off the plane and, after clearing the terminal, Phillipe and I went outside. I'd been warned that no one would be collecting us from Kuwait Airport, so we got a taxi to the hotel where the company had its office. It was a boring trip: the taxi driver couldn't understand a word of English, he had a full shemag on, and Phillipe wasn't in a very talkative mood. So, as we travelled, I took in all the sights of Kuwait. The places we passed made it seem that the city was a shithole, and it was.

After arriving at the office that afternoon, we were met by Tom. He told us that he was having a bit of a nightmare repatriating the sixteen Gurkhas who had been killed. If you've been killed in Iraq sometimes they won't release your body for a number of reasons. It can be a right pain in the arse. It's a delicate, painful enough process at the best of times, and you need, by law, to be repatriated. After our chat with Tom I had a good think about what I was going back to. I was too hyped up and had too much going on in my head to settle, so, after leaving Phillipe at the office, I took a walk along the beach. It looked beautiful under all of the lights.

I returned to my digs after my walk and watched a bit of TV, then clock-watched until breakfast. Phillipe had had no such problems, and had eaten and gone straight to bed. At 06:00 I went in and gave him a shake. I was still really hyped up and I talked to him about leave and what we'd both got up to. I guess I was trying to distract myself because I now felt the apprehension that I had felt when I went up to the north the first time. It was slightly unnerving. We went down and enjoyed a good breakfast. We finished eating and were ready to go through the rigmarole of getting back into northern Iraq, which was never easy. We collected our body armour and helmets and drove to the airport, going through the now familiar routines.

We cleared customs and boarded the Hercules wearing, once again, only our body armour and helmets. It was noticeably cooler. After another flight we were then touching down in Mosul. As soon as the tail was down we were out of its arse. Once everyone had got off, the tail went up and the plane turned around and took straight off again – not wanting to risk getting mortared or shot at.

Shortly afterwards, all the lads turned up to take us back to our base. Everyone was now wearing their winter gear and they complained that they'd had rotten weather. I could see for myself that the weather was shit. It was pissing down with freezing rain and I was beginning to think that maybe I should go back to Baghdad, where it was a lot warmer. And this was only November!

We had the normal mental dash across town and before long we were back at base. I went up to the ops room to see what the score was. Nothing much had changed while I'd been away, except the weather, of course. No one from our operation had been killed while I was away. There had just been a few minor injuries. This was good news. Fucking brilliant news in fact.

I quickly settled back into camp life. It was fast approaching Christmas (we were now at the end of November) and by this time we would more than likely have snow, which we did. I noticed all the expats wore gear branded as North Face (the outdoor-wear manufacturer). I wondered where it all came from and was informed it was all fake and was being sold at the airport. It was still excellent-quality Gore-Tex stuff, though, and it was cheap. Next chance I had I'd get some for myself, since it was now getting really cold.

I went for some food in the mess hall and then on to my room. The dog was hanging around outside my room and I gave her a pet. She'd grown a lot and now looked like a proper wolf. After a few minutes of fussing with the dog, who, for a change, didn't try to bite me, I went to the armoury to get my guns, ammo, radio and personal sat-nav. It was as if I'd never been away.

Tomorrow was a new day – my first proper day back – and I'd be a liar if I said that my arse wasn't giving it some. None of the guys who hadn't been away were fazed, but, because I'd been out of the country for a few weeks, I certainly realised how damn dangerous this place was. Once you've been here for a while you get used to it and it makes little difference. Today we had a brand-new mission to start. This was to be a new challenge and I must admit that I wasn't looking forward to it.

We were going to be travelling through some insurgent strongholds and this was going to be dangerous as hell. But what the fuck? In for a penny, in for a pound. And it's not as if we had a choice about which jobs we did – we just did what we were told to.

Chapter 10

Mass Graves

We were getting missions left, right and centre now because the military saw us as extremely flexible in our capability to carry out almost any task they threw at us. It was decided at the highest level that we would be given the most harrowing and, for me personally, the most upsetting and unsettling mission I've ever encountered or would ever want to.

Our new mission was to protect the American forensic scientists whose job it was to identify and excavate the mass graves that Saddam had created while trying to eradicate and exterminate the Kurdish people. These graves were scattered all over Iraq and it was going to be a tough task. However, our job was to protect just two of these mass-grave sites. The insurgents were going to be going balls out to stop the military, or us, aiding these scientists who were gathering evidence for the prosecution of Saddam Hussein. The evidence they gathered would form part of the drawn-out prosecution case that would eventually result in his execution.

This tyrant's regime had seen people whisked away from their homes in the night, never to be seen again. Saddam's men would go out and dig huge pits in isolated parts of the desert where they knew they could not be observed by any of the local people. These abducted people were then transported to the desert and segregated into separate groups (the men were separated from their families in one group and the women and children were put into another group). We knew this because when the scientists excavated these graves, they found them in separate pits. It's human nature that, when you separate or segregate a group of men and women, the men will rise up and fight to try to protect their wives and other loved ones; the women, however, will try to comfort their children. It's so very sad. This is what the scientist showed us in the first pit we came upon. There were women, children and babies in this pit and the women had all been shot in the back of the head with some sort of small-calibre weapon, probably a pistol by the look of it – a .38 (9mm) I was later told. The scientist said that they must have been subdued (like lambs to the slaughter).

The men, on the other hand, in the second pit (which was close by and far deeper than the women's grave) were just machine-gunned down. It seemed that they were desperately trying to evade execution and had all been torn down in a vicious hail of high-velocity rounds, which had ripped them to pieces. Obviously, a machine-gun post had been mounted on the side of the pit and just sprayed them with bullets, and they'd had no escape; though it seemed apparent that some of them had been trying to scale the sides of the pit when they were viciously mown down. All the bodies in this pit were in one corner, piled on top of one another, as the terrified and dying men had tried using the bodies of their dead neighbours as ladders to try to climb up out of the pits.

Even our hardened veterans of previous conflicts and atrocities had tears in their eyes; some of them refused even to go and look, and I can't say that I blame them. However, I felt compelled to witness this for myself, as it proved to me that the Americans had been right to finish Saddam's rule. It was truly one of the most shocking and emotional situations that I have ever witnessed and I hope never to see the likes of it again. It looked to me as if it was pure genocide. The terror that these poor people must have felt is unimaginable.

How anyone could have carried out such atrocities is beyond me. Killing men in battle against whom you're fighting is one thing; executing women, children and babies is truly barbaric. We were hardened mercenaries who had fought all over the world, and I knew most of us would not even bat an eyelid to slot someone who was trying to kill us; but the murder of women, children and babies was beyond comprehension. The sights I saw on that mission will truly haunt me for ever.

There were literally piles and piles of bodies; these poor, undoubtedly terrified, women still clutching their babies. Saddam was trying to ethnically cleanse his country, though genocide is probably a better word. As contractors/mercenaries, whatever, you try not to take the moral high ground, but it's so difficult sometimes. That fucker and all his henchmen deserved to hang.

In Iraq we had to work alongside some of the people who carried out these atrocities. Some were allowed to keep their positions of power in an effort to keep the peace. It was extremely hard to accept sometimes. Often you just had to walk away, take a deep breath and try really hard to keep your pistol in your holster, because sometimes the urge to blow them away could be almost overwhelming. Of course, knowing that you would get transferred or, worse, get sacked if you gave in to the impulse to slot the fucker was really the only thing that protected them from us.

It was, however, truly amazing how they had found these mass graves. One of the American scientists, who had a reputation of being one of the most knowledgeable and skilled professionals operating in his field, would use only local knowledge of the communities and the lie of the land. He had no electronic equipment to aid him and would be flown in a helicopter over the desert and could tell, from the air, where these mass graves were! He told us that he knew from experience which type of terrain was likely to conceal these graves. He said that land based in shallows, in wadis, places out of view were the most likely points. They also had to have reasonable access for heavy trucks. He told us that in certain areas, even after quite a few years, the graves could still be identified.

We were, yet again, going to be working alongside American troops on this mission. It made life a little bit easier having the backup of the largest military machine in the world.

Our first day on this mission started by running the gauntlet through Mosul as usual (trying just to get to this new job was a mission in itself!), then onto the main highway down to the southern area of northern Iraq. This road was like going down bomb alley, for it was a prime targeting area for the insurgents, and we were, yet again, very vulnerable, as we could be ambushed or encounter an IED at any time.

On this occasion, as we tried to get out of Mosul as quickly and safely as possible, it became apparent all was not well. Some of the streets became deserted – not a good sign at all, as it normally meant imminent attack or a bomb. *Boom!* The American patrol in front of us was hit, and hit bad. Must have been some sort of bomb, but we couldn't identify exactly what it was. All we could see was a burning, blown-to-pieces Humvee with burning American troops' body parts strewn across the highway. I saw a smoking boot with the leg still inside it. What could we do? We needed to get the hell out of that potential kill zone and it seemed that we were again in deep shit.

We carried on at breakneck speed and, fortunately, took no casualties. We all felt sorry for those Americans but we had to look after our own arses. They had armour and we didn't. We still had to complete our mission, as we were employed and paid to do so. We had to press on, but the Yanks were quickly on the scene with all their backup.

As soon as we got to the scientists' camp that morning, which was actually being protected by another PMC company, we went off to the mess hall to feed all our guys. Now this place had one of the best eating places in northern Iraq, but it was full of gung-ho American mercenaries just cleaning their guns on the tables (pretty rude, I thought, when people were eating). However, the camp was nice and, if we didn't like the conditions in the chow hall, they'd just tell us to fuck off and we would be on MREs again. And the Yanks do love their guns! They were also a nice bunch and in trouble spots around the world, I've always found the Americans to be very friendly.

We spoke to the forensic guys we were going to be looking after and we were all of the opinion that we should do a route recce with the Yanks first. We came to the decision that the Yanks had to go in first across the desert. They were planning on going through with their mine-disposal equipment. This was basically a big mineproof truck that would drive the route and, if it went over anything, no one would be hurt. We were pretty much getting sick of a lot of our guys being blown to shreds. The fact that we were losing so many men was wearing quite a few of the lads down, not surprisingly. No matter how tough or professional you are, it still hurts when you lose friends. After the mine detectors and mine incinerators looked after our routes, we could then move in. There were no rules or regulations on this job. We just had to ensure these guys had as safe a passage to their place of work as possible. We were chosen for this task primarily because of our immense firepower and four-wheel-drive off-road Toyotas. And we were good – damned good!

The route into the desert was pretty amazing and, just a few miles away from where these grave sites were situated were the ruins where parts of the film *The Exorcist* were shot. We drove past them and past the hotel that had been built to house the film crew. The hotel was abandoned once filming was finished and left for the use of the locals, though these were just Iraqi squatters. They moved in and took over and then had themselves a free hotel. This place looked very strange in the middle of the desert. It almost looked like the motel from *Psycho*. It was very bizarre. The ruins themselves were extremely impressive and we stopped to take a look around, but we had to be careful not to go inside because of the potential for booby traps.

But that came later. The task of getting these forensic guys from A to B safely was going to be tough. First, we had to be introduced to them – if they had no trust in us, the job wouldn't work. We ate with them at the canteen and built up a rapport with them. They weren't as nervous as we were about being shuttled around northern Iraq – civilians in war zones tend to be very complacent and generally too trusting, and they don't necessarily take into account what can happen to them. On one occasion in particular (later in our series of missions), they actually left camp on their own, with only a shadow of bodyguards, and one of their trucks was taken out big style, blown to bits by a big IED in the desert. A hard lesson to learn but a useful one – they had to be shown that you couldn't fuck around in places as volatile and dangerous as this without proper protection. They needed an education and they learned a tough lesson.

The camp they were living in was pretty luxurious compared with ours and very well protected. I think sometimes that because they were in the middle of nowhere they thought they were safe – but far from it: northern Iraq is rife with insurgents.

The places we were now operating in were safe havens for insurgents and they could easily adapt and hide in some of these remote areas to launch their attacks effectively and very efficiently. The insurgents had mines all over the place and this was one threat we couldn't avoid – it was out of our control. If you went over one of these, you were a goner. Even worse for us was that we had no way of finding or locating them.

After we'd eaten in their far superior canteen, we prepared to move. The first thing we had to do when exiting camp was to establish a roadblock to stop the oncoming traffic. This would enable the convoy to pass safely out of the camp gate – a critical part of the task. If any vehicle approached too quickly or wouldn't stop, it would be taken out.

Once we were rolling we'd be pretty much OK apart from the landmines and, hopefully, the Yanks would take care of them. The guys and girls in the investigation team were now part of our convoy and under our protection. On the first mission, we flew out of the gate, the lead vehicle with the .50-cal going out the fastest to get ahead and then to establish the roadblock. It was now game on – there was no turning back.

Following the death of our comrade, the Gurkha, in the incident with the mine, our arses were twitching constantly as we drove though the desert. As we travelled along these desert track roads, I had an unnerving feeling that these were the very same routes along which Saddam's men took those poor people to their horrific executions. At the same time as we were having this unnerving feeling along the route of death, you couldn't help but notice the remarkable scenery we were travelling through and, if you hadn't known it was Iraq, you could, quite possibly, imagine you were on a sightseeing tour of somewhere totally different in the world. Of course, you were soon snapped out of this. We put our shemags on to aid our breathing because of the desert dust.

One of our other big problems, apart from the shootings, bombings, landmines and breaking down, was getting stuck in the mud. This was more like quicksand and sometimes impossible to avoid. For this reason all of our vehicles carried towing chains. It was still a bastard of a job getting the trucks out but handy as hell having all these massive Fijians available to push as well. The biggest threat in the desert was the insurgent snipers. Some of these guys were very good and so we never underestimated them. They were highly trained, well financed and had the best weapons in Iraq (well, maybe not as good as ours).

The insurgents always seemed to have the upper hand. They had the hills and mountains, the cover and the local knowledge. When you were hit it was almost impossible to see the shooter, mainly because of the speeds you were travelling at and the type of terrain you travelled through. It's hard to identify targets at speed, especially over rough ground. It's even harder actually to shoot and hit them while you're moving.

As we got nearer to the grave sites I could see a US military Black Hawk helicopter and a large tented area. The Americans used to guard this place 24/7. It was feared that the insurgents would come and try to destroy the graves. As there were far too many bodies in these sites to remove, they'd probably have to torch them or blow them to pieces. Either way, it was evident that they were going to do their best to halt the evidence-gathering process.

Grim as it was, we had this job to do. We got closer to the Black Hawk helicopter just as it was starting to wind up and prepare for takeoff. However, when the blades started turning, the extremely fine excavated sand was blown everywhere and we couldn't see a fucking thing. We were also in the middle of nowhere, which didn't make things any easier: just desert, nothing else. But we couldn't see, so we just had to stop. We put more shemags on and then some eye protection and just waited for it to take off. After it had gone we still had to wait for all the sand to settle before we could carry on. We now were so covered in sand that it looked as if we'd been rolling in the stuff. It was made worse by the fact that we had doorless vehicles, but these vehicles were brilliant: they'd go through anything and take a hell of a lot of abuse.

Since Saddam's regime was overthrown in 2003, 270 mass graves have been reported. By mid-January 2004 the number of confirmed sites was up to 50-odd, and this would greatly increase in time. Some of the graves, not dissimilar to the ones we were protecting, were holding a few hundred bodies; some of the other graves went on for hundreds of metres and were packed with thousands of bodies. When we were there, 400,000 bodies had been discovered up to that point – this was by November. Amnesty International and Human Rights Watch claimed it could even be thousands more.

These people had gone missing over the past two decades. If those numbers proved accurate, they represented a crime against humanity surpassed only by the Rwandan genocide of 1994, Pol Pot's Cambodian Killing Fields in the 1970s and the Nazi Holocaust of World War Two. In the 1983 attack against Kurdish citizens belonging to the Barzani tribe, eight thousand of whom were rounded up in northern Iraq, the Kurdish people saw more of Saddam's regime and bore the brunt of it. These poor people were dragged screaming from their homes in the middle of the night and executed in the desert many miles away, and the aftermath of these bloodbaths was what we were witnessing.

To give you a greater idea of how much of a ruthless bastard Saddam was, in 1988, at the culmination of the al-Anfal campaign, approximately 182,000 people just disappeared over a very short period of time. They were later found to have been executed in the west and southwest of Iraq and were eventually found in separate mass graves (typically, men in one, women and children in another). This was the situation we had to face every day on this new mission – looking at what that bastard did to his own people.

That's not all. I'll give you a basic rundown showing the extent that this arsehole went to in order to get rid of people who stood up against his regime. He chemically attacked Kurdish villages between 1986 and 1988, including the Halabja attack when the Iraqi air force dropped sarin gas and VX and tabun chemical nerve agents on the civilian population, killing five-thousand people immediately and causing long-term medical problems for the survivors. There were later related deaths and was also an increase in the number of birth defects in a lot of the children. This pushed the eventual death toll up by thousands. It has been estimated that, altogether, more than a million Iraqis 'disappeared' under Saddam's regime.

There was a huge massacre in 1991 after Coalition troops pulled out and left Iraq. I was there and you could see the panic on the people's faces as we left. There were people in the streets screaming and pleading with us not to go. We had all felt bad at the time and we pulled out at night so we wouldn't have so much resistance from the Kurds; it was very harrowing. Saddam's men then went in and killed and maimed tens of thousands of soldiers and civilians for fighting for autonomy in northern Iraq after the First Gulf War. Truly sickening stuff.

The forensic scientists we were looking after planned to look at between eight and twenty grave sites and exhume the bodies, fully examine them and perform autopsies – then the case against Saddam could go ahead.

The country is still not stable, though, even to this day. So-called honour killings in 2006 saw around six-hundred women burnt, beaten, shot, strangled, thrown from tall buildings, crushed by vehicles, drowned, decapitated or made to kill themselves. I heard the story of a young girl who was stoned to death in a Kurdish village for meeting a boyfriend. This in turn led to a revenge massacre of twenty-three Sunnis in Mosul, where our main line of work was. This country was fucked.

As we looked around the graves it was amazing to see how these scientists could establish what had happened. It looked as if everything had been frozen in time. The bodies still had flesh on them, obviously from being preserved in the sand. You could still see the expressions on some of their faces – something I'd never like to see again. In my eyes the people *we* shot and killed in our gun battles brought it on themselves. We were forced to kill them purely out of self-defence. We were not executioners: we were just protecting ourselves.

Sometimes, after dropping the scientists off, we went out of the camp for a look around. This place could seem very tranquil and there were some beautiful ruins, as I previously mentioned, that we'd often stop at. However, we had to be careful because if we got into a routine the insurgents would suss this and it would turn into a mess. We'd normally leave the grave sites during mid-afternoon. Then, at around teatime, we'd get food at the scientists' camp (it was hard to get the Fijians to bypass any opportunity for food – they always wanted to stop). It was usually great grub.

Home time was now here and, after our feed, we all readied ourselves for the run through the north. We got on the main highway and went for it, driving as fast as we could. After around 15 kilometres we started to see some smoke – it was on the right-hand side of the carriageway. As we approached we could see two fuel trucks burning and the pieces that were left were riddled with holes. The guys in the trucks were well and truly dead. They'd obviously tried to run this route through the north without an armed escort (probably their employing company trying to save money) and these naïve guys had paid for it with their lives. There was nothing we could do for them, but we had a quick look at the area – mainly to see if the insurgents were still about – and we saw nothing. The insurgents had obviously hit hard and fast and got out of the area just as fast, leaving no trace. We carried on, leaving the smouldering wrecks and dead bodies behind us.

We arrived back in camp in no time, seeing just a few more bomb holes on the way. The adrenalin was always flowing while we were on the roads, but it was nice to get back to the safety and comfort of the camp.

After the normal rigmarole of unloading and yet more feeding for the Fijians, it was decided that we'd have a party/barbecue just to wind down and raise our spirits. We got all the booze out and some of the lads went up to raid the kitchens – they had to bribe some of the Yanks there with a few cans of beer to get us some fresh food to chuck on the barbie. Once this was accomplished it was game on.

We were soon all dressed in Fijian shirts (which were generally a bit too big for us) and the Gurkhas beheaded another goat – the last one we had. I was actually getting quite fond of that goat so that night I decided I was going to stick to the chicken kebabs. As usual for these occasions, we invited all of our American mates plus all the American women.

The Gurkhas had the whisky and the curry under control and had started to dance. It has to be said that their curries were far better than their dancing – they reminded me of the ladyboys in Bangkok! At least this time someone remembered to confiscate their kukris (knives) for the duration of the party, which in itself was no mean feat, as they don't like to be parted from them.

The barbie was well under way when, out of the corner of

my eye, I spotted a gorgeous American soldier – even better, she was female! I made a beeline for her and we soon got chatting. Her name was Suzie. It quickly became obvious that there was a mutual attraction going on. We were both pretty plastered at this point, as neither of us had eaten anything from the barbie; in fact it seemed as if everyone was having a good time and was a little the worse for drink. Suzie and I sneaked away from the party and went back to my little hooch for a private drink. Within minutes we had our kits off and we were going for it hot and heavy. We eventually made it back to the party only to find that it had pretty much wound down for the evening, but we managed to scrounge up some leftover grub from the barbie.

After our little escapade that evening a blossoming romance fell into place. It was great. I had all the excitement and adrenalin from my job plus the added benefit of having a romantic involvement and an even better way of relieving my stress! Suzie was a great girl, albeit that she was a sergeant in the US military. Romances in war zones rarely work out back in the real world but I enjoyed it while I could.

Chapter 11

Elections

Our next mission was probably the most sensitive, potentially dangerous and definitely the most complex we had yet had to carry out. As I said, we were flexible and could and would do any mission we were given, so we were tasked with doing the main security for the Iraqi elections – this was going to be no mean feat. It was, yet again, a dangerous, precarious job.

We now needed to take all of our guys training again, as this was going to be different altogether from what we had previously been doing. Most of them had never undertaken any task like this before. We had to train them in perimeter security and teach them search techniques. A lot of us British guys had done tours in Northern Ireland, so we were up to speed on all these procedures. This particular mission involved guarding a huge camp – which looked a bit like Butlins because it was an old holiday camp, but an Iraqi version, if you can imagine that. There were swings, roundabouts, slides, and even quite nice chalets. They had barbies, too – in fact everything that you would get in any holiday complex, except that this complex was in northern Iraq and we were now in control of it. Also, we had big fuck-off guns and were in the most dangerous place in the world. A very strange situation to be in!

The polling stations were going to be extremely tough to protect but the Yanks would be doing that. We just didn't have the manpower for it, and none of us relished the fact that these polling stations would be getting missiles or some other sort of deadly projectile fired at them at some time. The place we were in was going to be worse, however – far, far worse for us.

We had our white trucks, which had to be camouflaged. Nine times out of ten we had to be overt when carrying out our missions, but on this occasion we had to be covert. We thought about trying to get our hands on some black paint, but we just didn't have the time. We asked the US military if they could get us some, but, amazingly, they couldn't source any. So it was like-it-or-lump-it time. Then we were to place the trucks at regular intervals around the perimeter. We had all the country's leaders' ballots in our hands. This job could turn out to be mayhem, or not, but only time would tell.

There was a wooded area around the camp we were protecting, and this made for what was probably one of the scariest missions I've ever encountered. We'd had our white vehicles dressed in pretty crappy camouflage, which wasn't good. We just put as much foliage on them as possible so you couldn't see any white, or at least as little as possible. It was quite comical, actually, to watch all the Gurkhas hacking away at the trees and chucking tons of wood and branches on the Toyotas.

The local militia were very switched on and the Yanks were driving in and out of the Iraqi 'Butlins' in their tanks all day – it was truly an amazing sight! When they approach it sounds and feels like an earthquake. When a battle tank (which weighs over 60 tons) comes anywhere near you, the engines are so loud and the tracks they run on make one hell of a racket. You can feel the vibration from hundreds of metres away. The first time they passed only a few metres from me I nearly shat a brick, especially as they were travelling at about 40 m.p.h.! Every insurgent knew what the fuck was going on and we just hoped we had the upper hand.

Vehicles camouflaged (as well as we could, anyway), perimeter secured, everything was coming into place. We were preparing for a battle and, in a worst-case scenario, we would take the trouble to them if needs be. We had got wire cutters in place so that, if the insurgents did try to come through the woods, we could cut the fence and circle around any insurgents who penetrated the holiday camp and go on the offensive.

As soon as the fence had been cut we could penetrate the woods. This way they wouldn't be able to hide behind the trees and pick us off. It was that or stay as sitting ducks, stuck in the trucks, or taking some sort of cover and firing at shadows in the dark. Neither option was attractive. We needed to be able to get into the tree line. In hindsight, we should have got some camouflage fatigues from the Americans and posted a few of the lads inside the woods in covert positions, but hindsight is a wonderful thing. Anyway, here we were.

That was what we were all trained for. We'd all been in some of the most famous elite units and regiments in world – we could do this, surely. We certainly had the firepower and the training. If not, we were fucked. If we lost our stronghold on this place it could jeopardise the elections – just what the insurgents wanted – so we couldn't let this happen. This was truly a hardcore job.

On the perimeter, near the woods, it was pretty nervy, so we made a plan: at night no one was allowed out of their positions on foot – you had to be driven or you had to get on the radio and give your precise location and the direction in which you were moving. If anyone was seen walking around at night they'd be slotted (taken out). The ballot-box guys we were looking after were told this and, to make sure none of them tried to wander about at night, we posted a sentry on their accommodation.

This had to be done and was totally for their own protection – mainly because a lot of them were fucking idiots, I thought. There was bound to be some numpty trying to leave the security of their accommodation for a midnight stroll at some time or another, and we needed to prevent this. I came to the conclusion that most of them were thieving bastards and certainly couldn't be trusted. I'm not saying that all of them were bad, but there was certainly a bad element in the group.

We were pretty sure the insurgents would try to sabotage the elections at some point, so we could obviously take no chances, and, to make all matters worse for us, we were very vulnerable. All that separated us from the main highway through Mosul were 20 metres of woodland and a wire fence, which wasn't even barbed.

This place, looking like an old holiday complex that would have been at one time a nice place to stay, was very eerie. It seemed that the Iraqi people could have had a lot of fun here but now it was a kind of ghost town. It was all very sad, but very educational for me, though, because as you looked through the chalets, which were remarkably well equipped, you could come to the conclusion that, possibly, these people had a good life before Saddam and even during his reign. However, this holiday camp had obviously been deserted since the end of the war, as it was pretty run down. I found it all quite depressing.

The first night on the job was the worst for me. Once we had set our defences up, we just waited for what we thought would be an imminent attack from the insurgents. I was sitting in one of our Toyotas outside the accommodation reading a book. I was guarding the ballot guys. We had guys everywhere, so I could chill out. My job was only to make sure none of them wandered out.

Then, out of the corner of my eye, I saw some movement. Someone was coming across the now heavily armed camp. Fuck! I felt a surge of adrenalin as I rolled out of the door of my truck and got into a fire position. Obviously, no one had picked up on it and this guy, who was approaching fast, looked far too tall to be an insurgent! It turned out he was one of *our* fucking guys! I couldn't believe it. He came within a gnat's arse of getting his head blown off! I actually had my safety catch off and my sights on his head before I realised it was one of our guys. He was (would you believe it?) looking for some food. I think it was for some of the soup we had on the go. I had to explain to him that we were on lockdown and I really had to bang it home to the lads that there was a real chance one of us could get killed or badly wounded if we wandered about at night.

The trouble was that some of the guys were fearless. They'd been through so much shit already that northern Iraq didn't faze them any more. The fact that most of them were very religious didn't help matters either, because, once they had finished their prayers in the morning, they believed that God was protecting them and nothing could harm them, that they were almost invincible – obviously nothing could be further from the truth.

After about ten cups of coffee and through a miraculously quiet night, dawn broke and I went to check on the guys – who were all fast asleep! For fuck's sake – you could tell none of these guys were at all bothered about the situation we were in. Does that make them brave or stupid? You tell me. I gave them a bollocking and we got on with the job. If the insurgents got inside the camp we would be up shit creek. It would be a gun fight at the OK Corral for sure, and, with the darkness and staggered positions, we'd probably end up shooting a lot of our own guys.

Voters for the elections had to prove Iraqi citizenship and have been born before 31 December 1986. The elections were to be held on 15 December but this whole process could have gone on until March the following year if all didn't go well. Iraqis living abroad were also allowed to vote as well and the International Office of Migration set up polling stations in fourteen countries that had a substantial expatriate Iraqi population.

A total of 280,303 Iraqi exiles in fourteen countries registered to vote; roughly one in four of those was eligible to do so. Sixty per cent of Iraq's population are Shia Muslims, the rest are Sunni Muslims and Kurds. The election treated the whole country as one constituency. Political parties submitted lists of candidates and a certain number of names had to be a woman's. Candidates had to be at least thirty years old to be eligible to stand for election.

Parties or groups with militias could not run for election and nor could current members of the armed forces. Also barred from standing were former Ba'ath Party members (the political instrument of Saddam Hussein's rule). Still, it looked as though a hell of a lot of Iraqis were going to turn out and vote. We had a great deal of responsibility resting on our shoulders. If this went pear-shaped it wouldn't be good.

After returning to the perimeter and trying to explain to the guys how important it was not to sleep on the job, and after double-checking everything was OK, we all got some breakfast. As there were no cooking facilities available for us, we were eating MRE rations heated on a simple cooker – these MREs aren't bad, actually, and can be pretty varied. You can eat everything in them cold if you have to but they are definitely a lot nicer hot.

Once breakfast was finished, it was my turn to stand guard on the gate of the camp. We did this in pairs and tried to make the best of the limited cover we had. Still, it was pretty scary stuff. This morning I was there with my mate Dan. I took one of my guys' M240 GPMGs and slung it around my neck along with a belt of two hundred rounds of 7.62mm ammo. This thing could bring down a house, and, if someone tried a drive-by attack or tried to rush the gate, it would stop them. Also, I still had my M16. Dan was carrying his slightly smaller-calibre automatic weapon M249, but it was still deadly effective.

It was only white expats who worked the gate and the simple reason for this was that the dark skins of the Gurkhas and Fijians could sometimes confuse the US military, or at the very least make them nervy (never a good idea). So this wasn't a racial thing, simply that, if the US military saw a couple of dark-skinned guys, heavily armed and dressed in civilian clothing (as we all were), they might just get trigger-happy. So, to remove the risk to our guys, only the white expats would do the gate work at one of the two main entrances.

There was a big steel gate that we kept shut at all times, but had to open if an American patrol wanted to come in. The situation was quite intense because we were all very well aware that the threat of drive-by shootings was probable, so if the gates weren't opened quickly enough for the American tanks and troop carriers, they would, most likely, have ploughed straight on through them – these guys didn't like to stop for anything.

The ballot counters we were looking after were a right unruly bunch. They were constantly squabbling and fighting. It was not uncommon to see a fist fight. It made me wonder sometimes how the hell this country could ever sort itself out. Still, we were going great so far – no firefights, nothing – though I think the fact that we had American battle tanks trundling in and out on a regular basis had something to do with putting the insurgents off. However, if the insurgents wanted to, they could easily create an effective attack on our vulnerable camp. Fingers crossed that this wasn't going to be the case.

The elections were now approaching, starting the next day in fact, and the transport trucks turned up midmorning to take the ballot counters to their stations. We piled them all onto the trucks, all of them still squabbling. This is when I thought it was most likely the insurgents would strike, because, for sure, one of these guys would have a connection to, or could actually be, an insurgent. The insurgents could be sneaky bastards at the best of times and I wouldn't put it past them to try to infiltrate the group and strike from the inside. Our only defence, up to this point, was to keep constantly searching the counters on a regular basis for any kind of contraband, be it weapons, explosives or even knives.

Once the ballot guys left we had the camp to ourselves and we could all relax a little bit – have a bird bath and a shave maybe (the shower facilities weren't working, so we were roughing it).

The elections had a huge response with around 80 per cent of the population turning out. A lot didn't turn up because of the threat of violence, but it was still a good turnout, especially when you hear that only something like 61 per cent of the *British* population voted in the 2005 general election (and that was higher than in the 2001 election!).

We were now waiting in anticipation for the calls from the polling stations about any trouble, which we were sure was going to happen. Later that day, the calls started arriving – a lot of stations were attacked, but the overall picture was that the voting process was a success. People in northern Iraq really seemed to want change, and their huge turnout proved this. Change was evidently not going to be rapid in this country, though, and they are going to be shooting the crap out of each other for a long time to come. But we weren't employed to be ethnic policemen. Kurd, Arab, Sunni, Shia, whatever – if anyone had a go at us we would retaliate; we were there to do a job. We weren't ethnic social workers either. We'd seen violence on all sides. We'd driven past blown-up American Humvees with burning American body parts, which makes it hard not to pick sides or get angry, but we were mercenaries, pure and simple, and we just went where the money was.

There was a tactical problem we had with this camp we were looking after. Once you've been in a certain position for a while the enemy get to know exactly where you are and your numbers. They have lookouts posted and very good intelligence. The longer we were there the greater the threat. But we were guns for hire and no one cared about our welfare all that much (I tell a lie, though: some of the senior American officers really did seem to give a damn).

After the elections the ballot guys returned in their trucks and we started the process of getting rid of them, thank God – I've never met such a bigger bunch of arseholes. So when they eventually went we all breathed a sigh of relief and prepared to leave this holiday camp. We pulled all the bushes off the trucks on the perimeter and made ready to move. We pulled out of this Iraqi 'Butlins' as fast and effectively as possible. It seemed to work: we had no bother and not a shot was fired in anger at us. Of course, our reputation as hard, efficient bastards could have preceded us, but more likely it was down to luck. Whatever, our patrol was on its way back to the relative safety of a US military base and hot showers and some good food. We'd survived this epic. Now we would wait for our next mission, but we didn't know what this would be; we never did. Only time would tell.

We rolled into camp in typical fashion. Everyone expected

one of us, if not a few of us, to be towed in or to have been blown to pieces, but this time we weren't. We were all in one piece. Life was sweet. After our debrief I went to my pad and I chilled for a while, then went on the Internet to catch up on my emails. Then I went down the gym. The Gurkhas had a few shots of whisky and the Fijians went for food. All was good! The suicide squad had survived another mission, thank God! (*Whose* God doesn't matter – we just survived it.)

Once the elections were over and we had withdrawn from the Iraqi 'Butlins', I never did find out what became of that camp. Because of the state that northern Iraq is in, most redundant properties soon get occupied by squatters. Hopefully, this place could house quite a few people. It would be nice to think that a few poverty-stricken folk could benefit from what was a relatively nice place. The problem was that most people were still scared shitless at this time and feared change, because they'd been persecuted for so long. A lot of these people were so timid they wouldn't say boo to a goose. Still, if they haven't got hope, what *have* they got?

Chapter 12

Getting Injured

I'd been doing this job for almost a year now and I was feeling quite confident about it. I'd lost a few mates and comrades but I hadn't been injured, so I felt sure that it would never happen to me.

One particular wintery and overcast morning in November we were coming back from a routine mission and approaching camp when we came, yet again, under enemy fire. This time I wasn't so lucky, and a stray round, a 7.62mm (or it may have been shrapnel), hit me in the chest. My body armour stopped the round, or whatever it was, from penetrating my body but the plates in my jacket were fucked – totally smashed. However, the impact from that projectile broke six of my ribs, not that I knew that at the time.

I remember feeling as if I'd been punched in the chest and I thought, 'Oh God, this is it – fuck!' I was sure that I was a goner and I realised that I'd never felt so scared in my entire life. Then I felt a massive pain and then I felt nothing.

I regained consciousness some thirty hours later in hospital. I wasn't sure at first if I was still alive and it took me a few moments to realise that I was in bed. I was still in the north of Iraq and was in a US military hospital. I managed to attract the attention of one of the nurses and she came over to speak to me. After checking my vital signs she went off to fetch a doctor to come and speak to me.

The pain in my chest was immense; it was hurting even to breathe. The doctor came and told me that I'd been very lucky. Fuck me! I didn't feel lucky at that moment! He told me that my body armour had stopped whatever it was from penetrating my body, but that the impact had shattered or broken my ribs – hence the pain. He said that they were arranging for me to be transferred back to one of their hospitals in Germany and not to worry: I was going to be fine.

I lay there wondering what the fuck had happened and, more importantly, what had happened to the rest of my patrol. Were they all right? Was I the only one injured? The questions were racing through my head and I was desperate to see a familiar face who could tell me what had happened. I must have drifted off to sleep, because the next time I came round I saw one of my mates, Steve, standing at the end of my bed.

'Finally!' he said. 'I've been waiting for you to wake up, you lazy bastard.' I gathered my wits and then burst out with all the questions that had been preoccupying me earlier. He told me that I was the only injury and that my Fijian driver had just got the fuck out of there as fast as he could and got me back to base. He said that I'd had them worried but he could now go back and tell the lads that I was just lazing around in bed and would be fine.

The next day I was transferred by plane to hospital in Germany, where I spent the next few weeks recuperating. I had a lot of time to think about my circumstances and to decide whether or not to go back. I considered telling my parents about it, but then didn't, because I didn't want to worry them. I'd already misled them about what I was really doing out there and if I told them I was injured they would be frantic. What they didn't know wouldn't hurt them. In fact to this day I haven't told them, but I guess now the secret's out!

During my time in Germany I was extremely bored. The only light relief was from the nurses, who were friendly enough but were very busy – they had a lot of other patients to look after who were more seriously injured than I had been. I spent my days reading and sometimes talking to the other patients. I was bored stiff and couldn't wait to get back to work. All this idleness was making me feel guilty – about the lads I'd left behind and how they might be doing. I felt totally isolated and cut off from everything.

It was a relief when I was finally discharged and able to get back to Iraq. Now you may think that this is a funny thing to say, but I'd got so immersed in my life back there that I really was missing it, and I was missing my stupid dog Kasper and my patrol teammates. Call me crazy but I was itching to get back to it.

Chapter 13
Over Christmas

Christmas was coming, and I can't say that thoughts of the festive period were particularly gripping any of us. I'd been nursing some very sore ribs during my enforced time out. Most of us were single, so it really was of no importance to us. Sure, I'd miss my family (my parents and sister), but I wasn't really that bothered. I was now totally focused on this job – it was as if I had been encapsulated, as if we were all living in this bubble and the real world outside Iraq had pretty much faded away.

We cooked for ourselves quite a lot of the time on camp, and a few of the lads even had cooking hobs in their rooms. We often had impromptu barbecues, too. But it was a real treat for everyone when the Gurkhas cooked for us. Their speciality seemed to be curried goat – not sure if that was because of the availability of goats here or a genuine preference. The only problem was that the goat in question had to be alive!

Dirty Deeds Done Cheap

The first time I saw how they made their curry I was nearly sick. They would stand the goat up, stroke it to pacify it, and then, when it was calm and relaxed, one swoop of their kukri would lop off the goat's head clean off. The goat still stands up for a few seconds – as if the body hadn't quite caught up with the fact that it's dead – and then it falls over. This seemed really sick to me but I guess it was all right, actually, because the animal never knew what had hit it. After they had killed the goat they would skin it and gut it – that was basically all the preparation they did for the meat. Then the rest of the goat was just chopped up into more manageable bits – bones and everything. It seemed that the goat was in the pot and cooking in minutes.

The Gurkhas then created and cooked the most glorious of curries – everyone looked forward to one! The Gurkhas loved their curries, that and whisky! To encourage them to continue providing us all with these fantastic curries we even built them their own cooking area outside their accommodation one quiet afternoon.

Now, while we all were looking forward to this meal, we had one small problem: we now had to acquire a goat and, worse still, it had to be alive! We had a bit of luck here, as we needed to make a run up to Kurdistan near Turkey, so we thought that while we were there we would stock up on some booze and see if we couldn't buy a goat for ourselves! Once we managed to get one and had got it back to camp, we couldn't see the problem in keeping it alive for a while – after all we heard that goats will eat pretty much anything.

230

So the plan was try to see a goat farmer in the desert on the way back from Kurdistan, and buy a goat off him. Goat farming seemed to be just about the only life you saw out in the desert, anyway.

So, following our usual mad dash out of Mosul, which this time was uneventful, we arrived in Kurdistan and managed to grab the booze; now the only thing left for us to acquire was the goat! Once out of Kurdistan we started to scour the countryside for a goat herder; it wasn't long before we found one! As we approached I think he shat himself a little bit – he looked absolutely terrified seeing all these heavily armed mercenaries coming towards him. We managed to reassure him that all that we wanted was to buy ourselves a goat. He was so relieved he insisted on giving it to us for free.

Now this could have been a tempting situation but actually, with our own personal morals, we forced him to accept what the Gurkhas assured us was more than a reasonable price for the goat – I suppose they would know, it being one of their favourite foods. Their *absolute* favourite food, bizarrely I thought, was hot dogs!

Goat purchased, we had to get the thing back to camp. The only way to do this was to put it in the back with the gunner on one of the gun trucks and tie the thing up. It must have made quite a comical sight to any onlookers – that we had a live goat with us. The goat tried quite hard to chew and eat the gunner's trousers – much to the amusement of us all. We eventually managed to keep it away from our poor gunner, though not before it had nibbled quite a large hole in his pants.

The Gurkhas entertained us on the way back through the desert with a funny story about a village in Nepal where alcohol is totally banned because the locals there were known to be so fiery when they got drunk they had regularly got out their machetes and kukris and attacked each other to settle their arguments. We proceeded to drive back through Mosul with no trouble at all and the gunner, especially, was pleased to unload the goat, which by this time had also pissed and crapped pretty much everywhere.

The Gurkhas took the goat off and tethered it to a stake in the ground. Being a team leader, I was able to delegate the nasty job of cleaning out the back of the vehicle. But what the hell – you have to have a few perks, and asking someone else to clean up goat shit definitely counts as a perk! However, being an animal lover, I nonetheless still found it hard to see these things being killed.

Another interesting thing happened while we were in Kurdistan shopping for booze and our goat. We were wandering around the marketplace – not looking for anything in particular – when a mate called me over to a stall. He had just been offered a mini Uzi machine gun. This particular gun was about 8 inches long and looked immaculate, almost brand-new. The stallholder nearly shat a brick when Phillipe grabbed hold of it and disassembled it in front of him in seconds – to check that all the working parts were moving freely, that it was in order, was the real

McCoy and would actually fire. The stallholder wanted $250 for it.

We all gathered around and talked about it – it turned out that none of us, apart from Phillipe, had ever fired one of these guns before. We were all keen to try it out and we decided that $250 was a bargain, and if we all clubbed together we could buy ourselves a fun Christmas present. So we asked Phillipe to put the Uzi back together and we all turned out our pockets and managed to get the money together. We had to club together to do this because we never carried much cash with us – there was no need usually. The stallholder was now grinning at us, totally confident that he had made a good sale today. We probably paid more than he would have made by selling it to a local, but what the fuck! This appeared to be a brand-spanking-new mini Uzi and we were all raring to have a little blast on it and have a laugh. After all, we knew that you can't hit shit with these things because they're an open-bolt-action weapon and are so very short (hence notoriously inaccurate), their only advantage seeming to be the rate of fire you could put down. We decided we all wanted to try it out on the range. Just for a giggle, really.

Once we had scraped the money together we asked the cheerful stallholder for some 9mm ammo (these things eat ammo at an alarming rate, firing about twenty rounds per second). He grinned broadly and told us that he actually hadn't got any and we would have to look elsewhere. The git smiled at us and he wished us a good day. So now we had our mini Uzi but no sodding ammo – how fucking annoying is that? We decided that we might be able to scrounge some back at camp, so we left the market. I was looking forward to having a go with it and had visions of various movies I'd seen running through my head (unprofessional as fuck, I know). Yes, it all sounds a bit immature for a hardened soldier and now a mercenary, but all it was for us was a bit of fun and a bit of relief – nothing serious, just a giggle.

Christmas was almost here. We'd got our goat and an Uzi and we were feeling relaxed, but northern Iraq doesn't stop for Christmas, so we had to keep on our toes. Everything was now set for a good party – and then we received some bad news. On the camp a couple of miles up the road – Mosul Airport camp actually (called Marez) – an Iraqi employee had gone into the mess hall; he'd body-packed himself with explosives and coolly joined the most crowded area – the queue and servers – then detonated his device. His actions resulted in the deaths of twenty-nine US Marines and had blown a huge hole in the mess hall.

To make matters worse, this man had been a trusted employee for months and months, possibly over a year. He had even befriended some of the Marines he eventually killed. It is sickening, but it does show the power of religious beliefs when a person who knows you, whom you even think of as a friend, blows himself to pieces, killing himself and his friends. A betrayal like that makes everyone look sidelong at the local people working around them. It is so bad for morale with this underlying tension and unspoken accusations hanging around everyone. It was a terrible shock to all of us, as we had eaten in that mess hall on quite a regular basis – the Fijians needed feeding and stocking up all the time! It could easily have happened to us – a true shock for us all. The violence here never stopped.

I used to feel really bad for some of the American troops I met over in Iraq. A lot of them were there for the full eighteen-month tour – that's one hell of a long time to be away from your loved ones. I knew that the US military recruited a lot of its troops from within very poor or underprivileged areas of the US. Often, joining the military is the only employment these young men and women can get and they see it as a way to escape their life and an opportunity to travel and see the world. Often, they don't really expect to get posted to Iraq or Afghanistan, but in this day and age those are the main places you are likely to be sent. Most of the young recruits just want the easy life.

The US military appear to do this on purpose, because it's easier to recruit people from low-income communities than from the middle classes into the forces. The middle-class families have more options and are less likely to seek a career in the armed forces because the money is not that good. I am in no way slagging off any American troops – I have served alongside them many times with pride. However, you can't help but feel for these really young lads and girls, who had probably never left the US before and then they find themselves in one of these hellholes with real people shooting real bullets at them and really trying to kill them – and pretty often succeeding.

With Christmas coming up and our bosses trying to keep our spirits up, one of them thought it would be a lark to dress us all as Father Christmas (Santa Claus to our American friends). I don't think that the insurgents were going to find it quite as funny. So we approached the local tailors to see if they would be able to make up the suits for us. We weren't trying to wind up the Muslims or anything like that, just trying to give ourselves a little seasonal boost and hopefully have a laugh doing it. Now this may not have been the smartest idea we've ever had, but what the hell! We were just doing it for fun. The tailors we employed were all local Iraqis and they didn't seem to have a problem with making the suits for us.

The suits eventually turned up along with about a hundred Father Christmas hats for the Gurkhas and Fijians. I've got to say that the suits looked more than a little strange, as they appeared to be just big red boiler suits with a couple of Father Christmas logos stitched on the back (which wouldn't be visible once you'd put on your body armour, anyway) and they were shit quality as well. The hats were OK, though, and there wasn't time to get anything else now, anyway.

We got together to make the decision about when to wear them. It was extremely likely that over the Christmas period we could be locked down. That means we would not be allowed to leave camp. It was predicted that the insurgents were more likely to try to wreak havoc over the Christmas period, when morale among the Coalition forces was lower as people missed their families more. As it happened, the Americans did decide that attack was imminent and placed the camp in lockdown. No one was going anywhere.

It was decided to wear our Father Christmas outfits on any mission we could, because the object of dressing as Father Christmas was mainly to cheer up the Americans troops on camp who were really missing their families at this time of year. After all, we could choose to go home on leave at any time, but they couldn't. It should be a laugh for everyone apart from the Iraqis, who would probably have a total sense-of-humour failure. Never mind, eh!

We had only one mission over the Christmas period, and that was just to escort another security company across town. Mosul was so dangerous that we were often tasked with escorting other companies and sometimes even the US military across this mad place. Since we were financed by the Americans, we did whatever they asked of us. If there were no missions we would sit around camp, go to the gym, train, whatever. Over this festive period, even the American troops were going to limit their venturing out. The insurgents' offensive was building up and nobody was moving around much. We didn't *look* for trouble. If we could find the easy life, it was even better.

Our guys, however, were chomping at the bit, as we were all getting a bit bored, and to relieve this boredom we wanted to keep working. Most of us had an attitude of 'bring it on!' So, on 24 December we, the expats, donned our Father Christmas costumes and all the Fijians and Gurkhas put on their elf hats and we went up to the ops room for our brief. The guys from the other security company we were to be escorting that day couldn't believe their eyes. Here we all were, dressed as Father Christmas, wearing body armour and armed to the teeth, accompanied by the meanest-looking, best-armed elves you'd ever want to meet. They, on the other hand, were immaculately dressed wearing looks of total astonishment on their faces. They thought we were taking this piss, but you had to keep a sense of humour in this most dangerous of places in order to keep your sanity.

After the escort briefing we all mounted up and arranged the other company's vehicles in the centre of our convoy. We then proceeded to the entrance of the camp. Every American trooper we passed seemed to be in hysterics and clapped us as we went by. We certainly had put a smile on their faces (which had, after all, been one of the main points of wearing our costumes). We arrived at the main gate and the sentries were gobsmacked. 'You guys are joking, right?' was the question posed by the incredulous sentry. We just smiled and started loading up and generally getting ready for the off. They fell about laughing. At least we'd put a smile on a lot of depressed US soldiers' faces.

We tore out of the gate with the other company in the centre of our convoy. We were under no illusions that this wasn't going to be dangerous, and probably a lot more so than usual, as being dressed as Father Christmas wasn't going to help us: it could be classed as provocation. While the other company's men were feeling a bit bemused by our being dressed as Santa and his elves, we still exited in our normal style: safety catches off, ready, as always, for any eventuality.

As we cleared the entrance of the camp the other company, driving in their fully armoured, fully equipped SUVs, turned on their flashing blue lights (which were mounted in the grilles). We told them, in no uncertain terms, to turn them off straightaway. We didn't use this tactic, as it was bad for us, and, after all, we were in charge – this was why we had been employed by them in the first place, to look after them.

The US military wouldn't let these companies travel through the north at this time of year without the 'Father Christmas Protection Outfit', so what we said was gospel. If they didn't like our arrangements, they didn't travel. It was our mission.

Because the north of Iraq was so dangerous, we were often asked by the Americans to escort other PMCs in and out of these trouble spots. We now had what you could call a full military role and were called or nicknamed 'G Company' by the Yanks (unofficially, of course). We had a level of firepower that no other private security company had, or was allowed to have. We were packed with the best-trained guys you could get and the Yanks knew this and were always going to exploit it. Fair play to them: it would keep their own troops safe and we were, after all, there by choice and for the money.

As we sped through town we could see a lot of jaws dropping at the sight of us all decked out in our Christmas getup. It was funny if not a little embarrassing. I was a little concerned that wearing a bright red suit when there might have been snipers ready to take a pot shot at us was hardly a brilliant idea – nothing like making yourself an easy target – but, then again, even if we'd worn black they could have got us. The other factor that was slightly troubling me was the potential embarrassment of being taken out (injured or killed) while dressed as Father Christmas.

After we'd dropped off the other company at the airport, we peeled off and gave them a wave. The drop had gone remarkably well and without incident. We then headed back for a lovely relaxing evening and the prospect of our Christmas Day and the party; and we were also looking forward to a great, if a little chewy and bony, goat curry.

We had the booze, the Gurkhas' curry, music, barbecue and quite a few women from the American forces. I think the ladies found us a little bit more exciting than their male comrades and had made a real effort to befriend us mercenaries. Of course, the added bonus that probably won it for us was that we could get alcohol, which the American forces couldn't.

We bombed into camp that evening, then went through our usual routine of unloading and going for the debrief. After the debrief I returned to my hooch and took my

Father Christmas outfit off. Thank fuck for that! I was starting to feel a bit of a plonker and certainly looked like one, bombing around the most dangerous place in the world dressed as a kids' character – truly remarkable. Truly fucking stupid, but what a laugh!

I woke up Christmas Day feeling really great and a little bit squiffy. The weather was now fucking freezing but we were going to have a good time. We had no missions on, as the Americans had given us all the time off we wanted – well, a day or two, anyway. After doing admin all day, we sort of started our Christmas party. The American general in charge of the camp and his entourage were coming, so we had to hide all the booze. The Fijians were going to sing Christmas carols for the general, who seemed genuinely to love those guys. The beer started flowing and, of course, the whisky for the Gurkhas. I was looking forward to the evening, which I expected to be great. The Gurkhas already had the curry on the go, which I was quite relieved about – at least I hadn't had to witness the preparation, and that made the food more enjoyable to eat.

Party time came; the goat curry was smelling great; everything was good. We rigged up the sound system for a bit of music and all the American women and a few of our American mates turned up as well. The sound system kicked off and the whisky had been freely flowing all day, so the Gurkhas started dancing, which was funny as hell – though we probably should have taken their kukris off them before they started.

Just as we were getting into the swing of it, we heard the familiar noise of an incoming mortar. We all dived for cover in one of the concrete shelters. The mortar landed and embedded itself right next to one of our guys' hooches. It was stuck in the sandbags we piled up outside our doors for protection. I think God was smiling on us that night, because it didn't detonate. If it *had* gone off it would probably have taken most of us out and certainly would have ruined our party. We cleared the area for a while, as a precaution until we were fairly sure that the mortar wasn't going to go off, and then we removed the mortar and carried it to the perimeter wall and threw it back over.

Once the mortar had been disposed of, we returned to the barbecue and carried on partying. The curry turned out to be awesome, but it was a little hard to eat, what with the bones and gristle. We had a great night, though, drinking, dancing, telling stories, and quite a few of the lads pulled American girls and, from accounts in the morning, we gathered that most of them got laid that night.

We all woke up on Boxing Day with banging heads and generally feeling rough. On the bright side, we all now had a couple of days off and, with nothing to do, we all just chilled. It made a nice change not to be getting shot at.

Although we were still supposed to be on lockdown, we were soon asked to go on another mission. This was to be a route recce and none of us were that keen to do it. We agreed to go out but broke our rules by deciding to take an easier route than the one that had been suggested to us. After all, we had quite a bit of local knowledge by now and we knew that some of these routes would almost guarantee your getting shit in some form or another. Sometimes, when your nerves were wearing thin, you just didn't want to meet any trouble, and the route we picked seemed the far safer and better option. It was bad practice, but sometimes you do get tired of seeing comrades blown apart, so what the fuck! It was Christmas and we thought that changing the route slightly wouldn't make all that much difference.

We left camp and did the 'suicide run', as we'd come to call it, and proceeded north towards Turkey. The route we were taking was up through the mountains, which made it safer because this was Kurdish territory and we would, therefore, have mostly safe passage. The mountains were also fascinating and very beautiful – you could easily imagine you were on holiday, sometimes. We looked at our maps and discovered we would be passing some kind of monastery, so we decided to go and have a look, as we felt we were safe enough.

It was truly an incredible, stunning place. It stood probably 600 feet up the side of one of these magnificent mountains. There was only one road up to the monastery, which was a tightly curved switchback. We posted a sentry – who wasn't that bothered about seeing the place himself – over the lookout position and went up to have a look at this holy place. It was very beautiful and very peaceful. We all removed our body armour and major weapons, but we kept our pistols. We didn't really expect any trouble as we were almost at the Turkish border, so we all felt pretty safe. This was, after all, Kurdistan. It still felt disrespectful and wrong to be carrying weapons of death into such an obviously holy place but, while it's not nice, we had to be realistic and it was essential to remain to some extent armed. However, from here we could have seen anyone approaching from miles away. There was no possibility that anyone could approach from above: it was just too steep and there was absolutely no access that we could see.

I did wonder how the hell they had built this place. It beggared belief, perched as it was on the side of a steep mountain. Once inside the monastery we found that there were tunnels everywhere. They penetrated into the cliff itself, going in many different directions. It must have taken a lifetime to construct, and I thought it was pretty amazing. I really wanted to explore these tunnels but we didn't have the time. This beauty and the tranquillity of the place seemed like a safe haven to us, far better than facing the bombs and bullets back down in Mosul. It was very peaceful and calming. I remember thinking that maybe one day I would come back and explore properly, but, even as I thought this, I knew that I wouldn't.

We made our way out of the monastery and mounted up. A few of the guys had even managed to have a little kip. Everyone was feeling pretty chilled and we locked and loaded. As we were about to head off down the hill, we came across, unbelievably, a group of tourists: a couple and, presumably, their children. They were freaked out by our appearance, what with all the guns and body armour. We stopped for a chat with them. Once they had got over their initial fright, they told us that they were on holiday from Canada. I tried to explain to them that, although we were in Kurdistan, this was still a really dangerous place to be in and they were in very real danger of being abducted and held for ransom or, worse, tortured and executed. They didn't seem convinced, and we left them, shaking our heads at the absurdity of taking a tour into a country that was effectively still at war, with quite a lot of the insurgents trying to capture anyone not from Iraq. It was madness.

As we descended into this tremendous valley we were constantly thinking about this Canadian couple who were foolishly putting their children at risk. They had probably travelled from Turkey through Kurdistan, which, although a lot safer than Mosul, was still a very dangerous place. I was still worried about it and it played on my mind a lot for a couple of hours after. No sane person wants to see innocent civilians hurt or killed, let alone children. I wondered if I'd see them on the news; I half expected to.

We all felt a little calmer after looking at all this beautiful scenery and visiting that tranquil monastery. It was time to head back now, and we trundled off back down the hill, where, in all likelihood, the only real danger we faced was running into a sheep or a goat. But before long it was time to run the gauntlet again as we returned to Mosul.

Once back in camp, we could all relax, so we did our

usual hell-for-leather dash back and shot through town as fast as possible. We made it and fired on through the gate as quickly as we could. The American sentries, as always, gave us a wave and cheered when we came through – testament to the good relationship we had with them. We watched their backs, they watched ours – it was a cool understanding and, best of all, it worked.

We now had time off until New Year's Eve and we could do what the hell we wanted – except leave camp, as we were still on lockdown. We just chilled and enjoyed our time off.

Up to New Year's Eve it was pretty uneventful. We mainly did first-aid training, with our medics teaching the lads trauma procedures, e.g. treating basic gunshot wounds, trauma management and even how to apply a simple plaster. Medical training was essential because of all the contacts we regularly went through. We had suffered so many casualties and deaths over this tour that it had to be done. It was also essential in case one of the trained paramedics was taken out – we all had to have the basic knowledge to be able to patch him up the best we could.

So Christmas had come and gone, and here was New Year's Eve, and everyone was, to tell you the truth, getting a bit bored. There's only so much training you can do around camp. In Baghdad you were tasked daily, but up in the north (which was considered an insurgent stronghold) the Americans were very strict about movement. I'm not for one minute saying Baghdad was easy – far from it – but up in the north the insurgency was far more intense.

New Year's Eve was going to be our last day off, and then we would be in the thick of it again. We decided to get on the range again, just for a few hours at least. Mainly, we tried to put the guys under pressure with their drills. For example, as they were firing we'd shout 'Stoppage!' and instruct them to drop to one knee, take the magazine off, clear the weapon and get back into their fire positions. All this training, although mundane, was essential. The more range time we got, the slicker the guys became. Immediate-action (or IA) drills, as they are known, are essential.

We did, however, have an ulterior motive – the mini Uzi was still waiting to be tested out on the firing range.

We approached the American guy who was running our stores and requested a load of 9mm bullets. He wanted to know why we needed so many, since only a few of us carried a Beretta pistol. He said that he didn't have that many, so we couldn't have any. We told him about the mini Uzi and he grinned broadly and said we could have as many as we liked, provided we let him have a go as well. It seemed that the mini Uzi was something everyone wanted to have a go on!

So there we were on the range with this mini Uzi. We had managed to get a big bucket load of 9mm ammunition but this presented us with a problem, because we had only two magazines for this thing, and you could empty a magazine in under two seconds! So someone had to be loading all of the time. As we all wanted to have a go, this was going to be a bit of a pain in the arse. We all queued up and agreed that Phillipe could have first go. He let rip with this little fucking gun, eating up the rounds in its magazine in the blink of an eye. A little embarrassingly, Phillipe got only two rounds on target – and he'd used one before! It was only the 25-metre range, but this thing was missing its shoulder stock, so it was hard to control. We were all having a laugh at Phillipe's expense, but of course that had been the point – to have a laugh.

By the time it was my go I was in hysterics. I clipped the mag on and let rip – the fucking thing tried to jump out of my hand. These things had truly a rapid rate of fire and, unless you're less then 15 metres away from your target, forget it. Turns out that Phillipe was the best out of all of us. I managed only to wing the target – much to Phillipe's amusement. Because this mini Uzi didn't have a shoulder stock it was like having an automatic pistol and, because it's a very short-barrelled weapon, the rounds tend to go everywhere over a long range.

After the range practice that day, the Gurkhas cooked again and we managed to get hold of a load of wooden pallets from the store and built ourselves a fire for the evening. I was feeling a bit pissed off – call it a bit of depression if you prefer – but this was just down to the fact that I was away from my family. However, this was part and parcel of the job, so you had to just suck it up and get on with it.

Chapter 14
Final Leave

Having been hit and laid up for a number of weeks with nothing to do but think about what had happened to me and my mates more than I really cared to dwell on, I had wanted to go straight back to the job, since boredom was getting the better of me. However, my close brush with death and the ongoing casualty rate among our teams was really making me regret my decision to rush straight back to work. This job was tough and being injured had been a bit of a reality check.

My bosses had advised me to take some leave and go home and recuperate and really think about whether or not I wanted to continue. One of them pointed out that there is nothing worse than working with someone who is nervous and distracted with thoughts of his own mortality. A distracted person could easily endanger the lives of the whole team. At the time I was quite blasé about it. After all, I had been hit in the chest and survived – surely that meant

I was bulletproof. I had decided that northern Iraq didn't faze me. I had the attitude you should have after falling off a horse: you have to get straight back up and back in the saddle before your fears cripple you.

At the time that I went back to work I was sure that I had made the right decision and was eager to get back to all my mates. I was missing the camaraderie. After all, these guys had become my family. After only a few weeks back at work I realised that the advice I had been given was actually very good advice: I should have taken that extra time off to sort out my head and my feelings.

It wasn't long before one of my bosses suggested to me that I was burnt out and really needed to go home for a while. He was good about it. They weren't going to sack me or anything like that. However, they were concerned for my welfare and, for the safety of the whole team, I really needed to go home.

Initially I was furious about this. I felt almost cheated, as if I had been injured and come back and they were throwing me away. With hindsight, I realised the truth of what he said to me but at that time I was too angry to appreciate the favour he was doing for me. So, after stewing about it for the best part of two days, I reluctantly agreed to go home for some leave.

I had been working in Iraq for nearly fifteen months by this time and had taken only one decent leave up until this point so I reasoned to myself that I could go home and have time with my family and friends and then would be able to come back, clear-headed and focused. As soon as I told the boss that I would take the leave they arranged it so quickly that it almost made my head spin. In barely twenty-four hours I was, once again, packing up my stuff and hugging Kasper goodbye. Rotten dog still tried to bite me – that's gratitude for you! Once again I was transported to the airport by the Gurkhas. I said goodbye to all the lads, absolutely convinced that within a month I would be back and carrying on where I had left off. I remember standing outside the airport and watching them scream away with barely a backward glance. I picked up my bag and walked into the airport. After the usual delays I was once more on a plane to Kuwait. I had a twenty-four-hour layover in Kuwait, which wasn't so bad. I managed to explore a bit more and ate a couple of really good meals in the local restaurants.

The next day I was up early for my flight back to Amsterdam. Everything went really smoothly. There were no delays and before too long I was settling into my seat for the flight. I started to watch the in-flight movie but it was crap and I fell asleep really quickly. I didn't wake until the air stewardess shook my shoulder to get me to fasten my seat belt. After only about fifteen minutes I was once more in Schiphol. I had to kill about three hours in the airport before my flight back to Heathrow, so I wandered about the shops looking for a gift for my mum. I was feeling quite restless by now and kept checking my watch, but time seemed to have slowed to a crawl. Now that I was on my way home I couldn't wait to get there and catch up with everyone.

Eventually, after what seemed like eight hours but was really only three, the departure board showed that my flight was boarding. The flight to Heathrow was, thankfully, really short and before too long I was standing outside the airport thinking about how to get home. I hadn't told anyone I was coming back, so there wasn't anyone waiting for me this time. I decided to get the train back to Bristol and call my mate Rodders from the train and get him to collect me at Bristol Temple Meads station. The train was crowded and it was a struggle to find a seat, and, when I eventually found one, I found I was sharing with a harassed mum and her two toddlers, who were noisy and messy. I love kids but these two little monsters would have pushed anyone to the limits – shrieking and screaming and throwing tantrums. Their poor mum kept apologising to me for them but I was very relieved when she got off after about an hour. The rest of the train journey was pretty peaceful.

I got into Bristol, grabbed my bags and left the station. Fortunately, Rodders was waiting for me. We hugged and loaded my bags into his boot. We talked all the way home. I didn't mention my injury to him and, in fact, didn't really mention Iraq at all. Rodders, being quite a sensitive guy when it suits him, didn't push, realising that I didn't want to talk about it. He knew I would tell him if and when I wanted to.

Getting back to my home town was quite strange. There

was a new building in town that hadn't been there when I'd left. The whole place seemed somehow smaller than when I'd last been there. The quiet pace of life there was at such odds with what I had been going through for the past year that I wondered if I would find it too boring for me.

I spent a few days getting in touch with my mates and meeting up with them – mainly in the local. In fact I think I may have camped out in the pub for about a week. I guess I thought I needed it. I certainly know that I drank quite a chunk of my wages that week! As a lot of my friends are builders and mostly self-employed, they are able to take a lot of time off if they want to – so it was never a problem to find someone to hook up with and sink a few pints.

One evening, while I was sitting in the local (just for a change!) I bumped into this woman, Kim. I'd known her for years but never really knew her, if you know what I mean. She sat down next to me and asked how I was and said that she hadn't seen me for ages. I explained that I'd been out of the country for months and had only just got back. We were just sitting chatting when I told her that I hadn't had a shag for months and months.

She put down her drink and looked me in the eye and said, 'OK, your place or mine?' I had, unwisely, taken a big mouthful of my beer and I nearly spat it everywhere. She burst out laughing and blushed scarlet and said, 'Oh, sorry. Wasn't that a request?'

'Too damn right it was,' I replied.

I told her that I didn't actually have a place to call my

own at the moment, since I was crashing at a mate's. Once we'd both got over the embarrassment (I for asking and she for accepting with indecent haste), we decided to go back to her house.

Funny thing was, once we got there, she opened a bottle of wine and poured me a glass and we spent the whole night talking. We were still talking at about five in the morning and were both a bit more sober. Eventually, she grabbed me and dragged me off to bed. We had great sex and then fell asleep.

At about 9 a.m. Kim's kids (she had two, a boy and a girl) started banging on the door. I had totally forgotten about that – the kids had been in bed when we had got to her place the night before. I was really embarrassed. I buried my head under the covers as Kim got up and dressed and went downstairs to see to the kids. I lay there considering the best way to escape this compromising and embarrassing situation. I looked out of the window and briefly considered jumping out, but that would be cowardly and it was quite high. I got up and took myself to the bathroom for a shower. While there, I heard Kim knock on the door. She said she'd made me a cup of coffee and that I should come on down when I was done. I'd never been involved in a relationship with a woman who had kids before, so I was more than a bit nervous.

I couldn't stay in the shower any longer without turning into a prune, so I had to get out. I dried and dressed and came downstairs. Neither of the kids was there: her son had gone out to play football and her daughter had gone out to see friends. I was relieved. She then offered to make me breakfast and I gratefully accepted.

I was grateful, that is, until she placed my bacon and eggs in front of me. Ugh! Heart attack on a plate. I made a show of eating it while actually just chopping it up into smaller and smaller bits and pushing it around the plate. Kim laughed and said that she had many skills (she was a trained carpenter, had worked as a secretary, was a single parent and loved gardening) but cooking wasn't her strong point. She said it was because it was just another chore, like housework, and if you had to do it every day, three times a day, you would hate it too. I suppose she had a point but I, though freely admitting that I'm not very good at it, love my cooking.

Sex, though, was another of her skills, and, while Kim was chatting away, all I could really think about was that I wanted another shag – but I didn't have the nerve to say it.

Over the next few days I spent more and more time with Kim. She was a breath of fresh air with no airs or graces and barely any manners. Talk about blunt! Tact was obviously something that she had never learned. I found it quite endearing, as she was always brutally honest. I even got to know the kids a bit; they were nice kids if a little mouthy (like their mum I guess).

Anyway, we were both single and lonely and sort of just got on. I'd been dating her all of two weeks when I invited her up to London to meet up with some mates. I was due to go back to Iraq the next week and I wanted to be with her, but I also wanted to see my mates. We managed to sort out the logistics of work and childminders and off we went. We had a really great time: we did mega pub crawls and visited a few clubs.

We spent two really great days in London, I had a lot of fun with her and we laughed loads. However, all good things come to an end, and we had to return home – Kim had to take her kids to school, among other things.

We caught the tube to Paddington but found that we had about an hour to kill before our train, so Kim challenged me to a game of pool. Now I fancy myself as a bit of a pool player, so I was well up for it. We got down to dares and bets or forfeits should either of us lose. I've got to say I had the best game of pool in my life. She is such a cheat and she totally stuffed my arse. She does not play fair.

She can play really well but her distraction techniques when it was my go won every time. She danced to the music over the pocket I was aiming at. Then she'd pretend to be uninterested and plant her arse over the pocket with her back to me. She has the greatest arse I've ever seen and knows how to use it! I lost the game! I can't remember what our bet was, but she won –it was the best game of pool ever.

We had a few drinks riding on each game while we were waiting. She stuffed me but I've never been happier to lose a game! Time was short and we were having fun. After about an hour our train was due, so we grabbed our bags and legged it – of course, we'd left it a bit late and we were a bit the worse for our vodka-shot bets, which I'd mostly lost. But she still kept pace with me. What a woman!

So we were finally on the train and just talking about things we had always wanted to do before we were forty years old. Kim produced a pack of cards and challenged me to a game – for forfeits. So I said that I'd never had sex on a train. Fuck me if she doesn't turn around and say 'OK, next hand for sex on the train or not.'

Now she had been totally stuffing me: she'd already won about 5–2 on rummy (I'm sure she cheats, but I don't know how!). So my prize was sex on the train. It was such a tense game but she dealt me a flush and I only needed two cards to win. I couldn't believe it when I beat her. She went absolutely crimson and tried to squirm out of it. I was triumphant and gloating and winding her up. So she says she needs a drink. OK, I thought. I hadn't really expected her to come through, anyway, but the gloat factor was well worth it.

So, leaving our coats and bags on the seats, we made our way up to the buffet car. It turned out we hadn't got much change between us and would need to go to the cashpoint at the station, so we barely managed to scrape the cost of a vodka. I needed the toilet and left Kim to get the drinks.

There was a young lad with his bags sitting near the entrance to the toilet. I went into the little cubicle. I was quite happily having a piss and sort of whistling to myself when the door suddenly burst open – I jumped out my skin and turned to find Kim shoving me out the way so she could shut the door behind her.

'Well I'm here,' she said. I was so shocked I peed all over the toilet seat. Shit, shit, shit! I was thinking. Fuck me! This woman's great. I managed to finish my pee and Kim very kindly wiped up the accidental spillage!

Now you have to understand this cubicle wasn't one of those nice big ones with the circular doors. No, this was an old-fashioned one – with a door with a small bolt-type lock – and really small (like that of a plane loo). So we're both squeezed in and she starts to tell me this story about how the nice man on the buffet counter gave her the Coke for free because she didn't have enough change. I was totally unable to understand what the fuck she was on about, and then she hangs her coat on the peg and says, 'Well? How about it?'

She undid her jeans and pulled them down, then her pants, and, after cleaning the toilet seat and lid with wipes, bent over and presented her fantastic arse to me. Well, what could I do? What would you do? I went for it. No, *we* went for it. The train was going at about 60 m.p.h. and I think we even stopped at a few stations. I could see people walking past the window but, fuck it, we went for it.

People knocked on the door but we ignored them. I took my T-shirt off and dumped it on the sink. Kim kept saying, 'Pete, sink!' It took me ages to twig that the sink had one of those automatic taps and I'd dumped my T-shirt in it; the tap had come on and was soaking my T-shirt and jacket. I grabbed it out and threw it on the floor. We carried on. Somebody knocked on the door just as I was about to come. How fucking frustrating is *that*? Talk about offputting!

Kim was sort of kneeling over the toilet but we could see each other's faces in the mirror. We stared at each other as we fucked. Her head was banging on the side of the cubicle but I really didn't care. God, this was so fucking horny. I came, and took a minute or so to calm down, and Kim was trying to move when I realised that, no, I wasn't done. I was going to come again.

That was it. We started again. It was the most dirty and erotic thing I've ever done, a real knee trembler. But, fuck me, you should try it.

So, thirty minutes later, I'm trying to put on my soaking-wet T-shirt and hoping to look casual (not really succeeding, I found, as Kim collapsed into fits of giggles). We came out of the toilet, Kim first. She looked around. There was nobody. Strange, that! She gave me the all-clear and we returned to the carriage and our seats, where we'd left our coats.

As we were heading back to our seats a guy looked at me and smiled knowingly. I just grinned back! I didn't give a damn about embarrassment – I was feeling too good!

The train was just pulling into a station and a woman got up from sitting on Kim's coat and Kim had the nerve to say something – we'd been gone nearly thirty minutes! We sat down and Kim produced the vodka and the Coke and cups. We poured ourselves a drink and burst out laughing. Both of us were unable to believe what we'd done. What a memory!

Then Kim lifted her eyebrow and gave me a sly look. She got the playing cards out of her bag, started to shuffle them and said, 'So, what's the bet this time?' We both burst out laughing and Kim dealt again while we both tried to go one better, suggesting the most outrageous bets we could think of. It was such a laugh, and I'll never forget it.

Later that night, once we'd arrived back home, I was cuddling Kim in bed when I realised that I was having the best time with her. The adrenalin rush that I had previously only got from doing my dangerous jobs was nothing compared with the adrenalin rush I got from spending time with this woman. The most exciting thing I had ever done was that risky shag in the train loo!

I began to question the wisdom of returning to Iraq. I was really falling hard for this crazy woman and if I went back to work I might well get killed or seriously maimed. I might never have the chance to pursue this relationship to the end.

I didn't know when the end of this relationship was going to come but I knew that I wanted more. She was more exciting and fun than getting shot at in Iraq, that was for sure. I still hadn't really told her what I was doing for a living. She had assumed that I worked for an oil company on the oil rigs, which I had done, admittedly. I thought that she would probably be disgusted, as she was quite anti-war and against guns. I love the action, my guns and, of course, the money, but I thought I might well be falling in love with this woman. Hmm, guns or love? I would need to consider seriously whether or not to go back to Iraq. I had only about a week left and I had been planning to go up and visit my parents, but I didn't want to leave Kim.

I eventually persuaded her to come with me to visit them.

We travelled by train but there was no repeat performance of the toilet gymnastics, since we had to take her son with us. Nevertheless, we still had a really great time with my parents and even Morgan, her son, was entertained. My parents were gobsmacked because I'd actually brought a girlfriend up to visit them, and not only that but a girlfriend with children!

Kim and my mum got on really well. They have a lot in common, anyway. After spending a long weekend with them and returning to the West Country, I was even more conflicted about returning to Iraq. Would I regret it if I went? Would she find someone new? Would I feel the same way with distance?

I was down to three days until my scheduled return when I realised that I wasn't going to go back. I was sorry that I wouldn't see the guys again but realised that it was time to actually start to live my own life, for me. I could envision this future with Kim. I'd never imagined that with any woman before, so I was really keen to carry on.

After much soul-searching I decided that I had done my time in Iraq. Next time I might not be so lucky, and it was time for a change. I was qualified for rope access work and bodyguard work, but decided that rope access work was the way to go. I rang around and had soon found myself another position with an oil company. All this while Kim was none the wiser, which made me feel a little guilty about deceiving her, but I convinced myself that I would tell her the truth eventually – not now. I hoped to have a more secure relationship before I told her what I had actually been doing.

After I'd spent nearly eighteen months with Kim we got married. I never returned to Iraq and I can't say that I'm sorry. I don't regret going there in the first place, but I'm just thankful that I came back in one piece when so many of my friends didn't. I know that I made the right choice and I eventually came clean with Kim. She was remarkably understanding about the whole thing and had heard gossip about me, anyway.

I now work in the oil industry as a rope-access technician. It's boring as hell – the hours are long and the working conditions are not only grim but soul-destroying, but I know now that I would rather be alive to spend my free time with my new family than return to that sort of dangerous situation ever again. Besides that, I don't think Kim will ever let me go back. Of course, I could always lie, which she tells me I do quite well, but I know that she would see straight through it.

However, as I've been writing this book, I have been offered work in Baghdad, so I can't honestly say I *won't* go back. Hmm, have to think hard – the money isn't what it was but it's still more than I can earn in the oil industry, and it's far more exciting. Not sure about my chances of convincing Kim that it's worth it. We shall see . . .

Glossary

blue on blue:	action, or 'friendly fire', by allied or friendly forces, mostly accidental (a blue-on-blue situation)
bootneck:	Royal Marine Commando
click:	distance of 1 kilometre
comms:	communications equipment
contact:	when you come under effective enemy fire
debus:	get out of your vehicle ASAP
50-cal:	.50-calibre heavy-duty machine gun
GPMG:	general-purpose machine gun
Herc:	Hercules aircraft
hooch:	personal room/accommodation
Humvee:	military utility vehicle (abbreviation of 'high-mobility, multipurpose wheeled vehicle'); also called Hummer
IA:	immediate action (e.g. an immediate-action drill)
IED:	improvised explosive device

intel:	intelligence, information
MRE:	American forces' ready-to-eat emergency food rations (stands for 'meal, ready-to-eat')
ND:	negligent discharge (of a weapon)
PMC:	private military contractor
PSD:	personal security detachment
Route Irish:	Baghdad Airport road, a 12-kilometre stretch of road that links the Green Zone to the airport
RPG:	rocket-propelled grenade
RV:	rendezvous point
scran:	informal word for food, commonly used by military personnel
SAS:	Special Air Service
SBS:	Special Boat Service
shemags:	veils that foreign forces use to protect their faces from the sand
SUV:	sport utility vehicle
2IC:	second-in-command
VCP:	vehicle checkpoint